THE BLACK COUNTRY GOOD BEER GUIDE

CW00557747

Edited by David King
Layout by Andy Parton
Compiled by the Black Country branches
of the Campaign for Real Ale:
Dudley, Stourbridge, Walsall and Wolverhampton

Produced by Waterloo Design & Print plc,
Reliance House, Birmingham Street,
Halesowen B63 3HW

**CAMPAIGN
FOR
REAL ALE**

Published by the Campaign for Real Ale Ltd.,
230 Hatfield Road, St Albans, Hertfordshire AL1 4LW
Tel: 01727 867201. Fax 01727 867670.

How to use this guide

Locality	**Dudley**
Pub name	**Bottle & Glass**
Address	**Black Country Living Museum, Tipton Road, DY1 4SQ**
Opening hours	⏱ 12:00-17:30 Mon-Sat; 12:00-15:00 Sun
Telephone no.	☎
Draught beers	**Holden's Bitter**
Pub description	Originally located in Moor Lane, Buckpool, Brierley Hill, this building was moved brick-by-brick to the museum, as were its neighbours. Open only during museum opening times and to its visitors, this picturesque old pub features on the front cover of the Black Country Good Beer Guide.
Facilities	♨ Q ⊟

Key to symbols

♨ **Real fire:** a fire fuelled by coal, smokeless fuel or logs

Q Quiet pub: free from piped music, jukeboxes, electronic games and TVs (at least one room)

☎ **Family room:** where the licensee guarantees that families are warmly (and legally) welcome in their own separate room, not a corridor or a corner of the main bar or lounge

✿ **Outdoor drinking area:** this may vary from a garden to benches on a pavement

☞ **Accommodation:** rooms to let (no assessment of quality or price is made)

◀ **Lunchtime meals:** not snacks but substantial fare (including one hot dish) and in the pub itself, not in a separate restaurant

▶ **Evening meals:** as for lunchtime meals; separate restaurants are often mentioned in the pub description

⊟ **Public bar:** a traditional public bar, where the beer may be cheaper

♿ **Wheelchair access:** easy access to the pubs and WCs

⇄ **Near railway station:** within half a mile: the name of the station is only given if it differs from the town itself

⊖ **Near Metro station:** within half a mile

♣ **Traditional pub games played**

🍎 **Real draught cider** (not keg cider) available

P **Pub has its own car park**

⊗ **No-smoking room or area:** a specially designed smoke-free zone, available to drinkers and not just diners; this may range in size from a few tables to a whole bar

Ⴎ **Oversized lined pint glasses:** used for some or all beers

Every effort has been made to ensure the accuracy of the information in the Black Country Good Beer Guide, but no responsibility can be accepted for errors and it is inevitable that some pubs and breweries will change their character during the currency of this guide. Opening times may also vary from the guide.

Foreword

I first saw the attraction that locally brewed real ale had when I worked in the Old Vic in Dudley as a barman. I saw too the contribution it makes to Black Country culture and the importance the industry makes to our economy. And I have seen at first hand the fantastic job CAMRA does to support and promote local beers.

Like many, I went though my 'lager stage' when I mistakenly thought that beer had to have a fizz! On returning to Dudley after University, I discovered real ale in local pubs, like Bathams' Lamp Tavern, Ansells' the Old Vic, the legendary Olde Swan in Netherton and the pubs in Gornal and Woodsetton selling Holdens and Simpkiss, now recreated by the Enville Brewery.

Local beer always had a distinctive taste and Black Country pubs also had a 'feel' that is not found in many places - a confidence that the area does not have to feel second best to anywhere for its beer and pubs.

My upbringing in an area so famous for its small breweries and unique pubs affected the way I thought about the industry when I went to work at the Treasury in 1999, where I was able to play a part in the duty cuts we introduced to help small brewers.

Since then, after I became MP for Dudley North, I am proud to say that I have supported CAMRA's campaign for the full pint and played a part in enabling other MPs to sample our delicious local brews by getting Holdens' served in the House of Commons.

Many often forget in these days of the burgeoning micro-brewing industry, that in the 1980s and early 1990s, the Black Country was known as an oasis for independent brewing from the 'Big Six' national breweries. Thankfully, real ale is now far more popular and the area remains a centre for brewing quality bitters and milds.

The Black Country has a proud history of brewing quality beers and providing friendly and welcoming pubs. Long may it continue to do so. Enjoy your time in the Black Country and do try to visit some of the many and varied attractions as well as its pubs.

Congratulations to everyone at CAMRA on your many successes to date and best wishes for the future.

Ian Austin
MP for Dudley North

Introduction

Welcome to the first Black Country Good Beer Guide of the twenty-first century. We hope that you will find it both a useful reference source and an enjoyable read.

As traditionalists will tell you, the area that this guide covers is not strictly speaking the Black Country: our guide extends a little further in some directions. Four branches of the Campaign for Real Ale have been involved in the thirsty research for this guide: Dudley, Stourbridge, Walsall and Wolverhampton. Each branch has members and pubs that fall within the Black Country, but we have also included pubs from the rest of the West Midlands county that each branch covers. If this seems a liberty, console yourself with the knowledge that you are getting more pubs for your money.

CAMRA members have surveyed each pub included in this guide and all sold good quality real ale at the time of the survey. No payments have been accepted for inclusion and no advertisements have been accepted from pubs.

We are fortunate that even through the era of keg beer, when you could buy fizzy pints that claimed to help you excel and to work wonders, the Black Country and surrounding area maintained a tradition of real ale. Many large and family breweries continued to supply their locals with real ale and some continue to do so today.

At the end of the guide we have provided details of some of the local breweries that serve this area. You will find that some listed pubs have beer from further afield, but CAMRA's annual Good Beer Guide will provide you with the most comprehensive details you can find.

The quality of beer can be affected by changes in ownership or staff. This is because, as you can read elsewhere, real ale is a live product and requires some skill not only in its production but also in its storage and delivery. We will notify you of any updates to this guide on our web site: www.blackcountrygoodbeerguide.co.uk and we would be pleased to receive your comments on any pubs that you think should be added to or removed from our list.

Not every pub selling real ale in the area is in this guide. We worked from a starting point of not providing a list of real ale pubs in the area, but instead to offer you a list of pubs that we can recommend. When branches send their pub lists to HQ for the annual national guide, most branches have to omit some good pubs because there is a limit on how many each can submit. There were no number limits on this guide: just quality limits. We may have inadvertently missed a few gems but we hope not.

I would like to thank all of the people who have contributed to the production of this guide. Our first meeting was over a year before final publication. Each branch took their turn to arrange a meeting in one of their favourite pubs and when we had been to each of the four areas, we started again visiting another set of pubs. (And you think compiling one of these guides is easy!) Andy Parton merits particular mention for assuming the role of typesetting this book, as does Gavin Lawson for his fine maps. We are also grateful to David Mawdsley and the staff of Waterloo Design & Print plc., for their help and advice in the production of this guide; to Jon Raven, for the recipes from the Book of the Black Country, published by Broadside; and to the Black County Museum for access to take the cover photograph. At each meeting, I have been impressed by the friendliness of the people from each branch and how knowledgeable and passionate they are about the quality of what they drink.

If you care about the quality of what you drink, join the Campaign for Real Ale.

If you are a CAMRA member but you are not active, try helping for a couple of hours at a beer festival. That's what first got me involved after three years of being no more active than reading my What's Brewing newspaper each month.

If you like wine as much as beer, well so do I, as do many other CAMRA members. You can be just as analytical and flowery describing beer as you can wine, if that's what you like. There are beers for delicate sipping, just like wine, and most beers go with food just as well as wine. There are also, thankfully, beers such as a delicate traditional Mild, that are just bostin' when you want to drink quite a few pints without becoming senseless, or you need to dampen the fire of a good curry.

Beer is our national alcoholic drink and it is worth appreciating how lucky we are as we sup beer from a good brewery and a good pub.

Cheers and good health.
David King
Chairman of the Black Country Good Beer Guide Production Committee.

Young Members

When the Campaign for Real Ale started back in the Seventies, many young people joined, grateful for an alternative to the metallic fizz of Red Barrel and Double Diamond: two heavily promoted mass-produced keg beers. Sales of lager were still modest and supermarkets were starting to encourage the British to try wine.

Pubs were simple places, what we might call 'traditional' in the twenty-first century. Drink was cheap and the choice was much less than today: usually between two or three beers, wine or spirits with mixers.

Nowadays, there are dozens of drinks aimed at young people and it suits the marketing companies to portray pubs and real ale as old-fashioned. Just as processed food has a higher sugar content than it did thirty years ago, so does drink. The profits are higher on processed food and drink and so the marketing industry targets young consumers with sweeter value-added products.

So if there is a tendency for the average age of CAMRA members to increase year-by-year, how do we keep the brewer's art alive and appreciated by tomorrow's consumers?

One way is for the lovers and makers of real ale to target young consumers. I recently gate-crashed a group of West Midlands CAMRA Young Members on a tour of the Sarah Hughes Brewery in Sedgley, to find if and why they are ignoring alcopops and the various vodka-based drinks on sale.

Young CAMRA members on brewery tour

It was reassuring to discover that the main reason for preferring real ale over other drinks is to do with Quality. The gassiness of lagers brewed in the U.K. was a common criticism among the gathered young persons, along with its lack of taste. Having enjoyed a tour of the Sarah Hughes brewery, the group were exploring the diversity of real ales on sale in the bar. "Lager doesn't have the variety of taste that real ale has", said one enthusiastic drinker.

Looking around the pub, there were a worrying number of middle-aged people in the pub drinking lager: remarkable in a homebrew pub, but perhaps a testament to the power of advertising. I remember a cider pub in Birmingham and a small brew pub in Dudley that allowed national brands onto their bar and subsequently sales of their own brands sharply declined. Faced with busy bar staff and only a few seconds clear sight of the bar taps, most customers will tend to go for the name that they recognise.

I asked the CAMRA Young Members if they felt that they are the target of the advertising of alcohol. Several felt that drink advertising is actually targeted at consumers younger than eighteen, with alcopops being pushed in bars more than lager. The sweet and fruity drinks, often loaded with a high percentage of alcohol, are designed for the inexperienced palate. There is often an underlying message that encourages a drink to be bought for its high alcohol content rather than the enjoyment of the drink itself. Real ale is seen as unfashionable.

Supermarkets also encourage the consumption of low quality alcohol drinks, with tinned lager and foreign beer being heavily discounted in favour of the few bottled real ales that most supermarkets do carry. Finding bottle-conditioned beer in supermarkets is not easy, though the CAMRA Bottled Real Ale (BRA) scheme has proved successful. Many bottles now carry the logo shown on this page.

The price difference between tinned lager and bottled real ale is much greater than lager and beer in pubs, and price is a particular concern amongst young drinkers. One member showed me a loyalty card given to him in a student bar one night. If you bought three pints of a certain brand of lager, you got a fourth free. This would seem a useful marketing idea that real ale brewers might adopt.

So, the good news is that there are young people out there who take the time and trouble to learn and care about what they drink. They can taste the differences between beers and are keen to learn more. Local branches and beer festivals might consider arranging tasting sessions for under-25s, and retailers might consider marketing real ale at younger people.

Meanwhile, if you are among the younger end of the age spectrum and you have considered joining CAMRA, helping at beer festivals or just learning more about real ale, do make contact with your local branch. All Black Country branches have their own web site and have monthly meetings and social events. They will be grateful for your input.

What is Real Ale?

CAMRA defines real ale as living beer that is matured, stored and served under natural conditions.

The beer is normally brewed from the traditional ingredients of hops, barley, water and yeast. It is fermented in large containers then put into casks or barrels where it ferments again while being stored.

The secondary fermentation will conclude in a pub's cellar and when it is ready to be served, it is pumped from the cellar to the bar using hand pumps or electric pumps. Or it might be poured straight from the cask into a jug or glass. It will not be forced from cask to tap by the use of gas pressure.

Isn't all beer real ale?

No. It's a bit like the milk you get in little cartons at snack bars compared with the milk your milkman brings you. The stuff in the little cartons last for weeks until it is opened, whereas the milkman's milk goes off quickly because it is more natural.

Beer can be made to last a long time by killing off the yeasts prematurely. Then, like UHT milk, it can be stored and delivered less carefully; but just like UHT milk, keg beer and most U.K. lagers just do not actually taste as good as the real thing.

"Cream flow" and "smooth flow" beers are processed keg beers that have nitrogen forcing it through the tap to fizz it up and give a creamy feel in the mouth. The same technique is used in the cans of beer with a "widget" that explodes when you open the can, again forcing nitrogen through the beer. The best thing you can say about these mass-produced heavily advertised products is that they are consistent. With so many pubs and clubs offering indifferent products and, even worse, badly kept real ale, it is easy to see why so many people prefer the consistently mediocre to bad or unreliable.

Real ale takes skill to make, skill to transport to pubs, and then requires yet more skill to store and to judge when it is ready to be served. As every stage of the process is important, quality assurance schemes such as the Cask Marque also include the delivery stage in their scheme.

So, when you drink a really good pint, compliment the landlord, and when you are sold a bad pint, take it straight back to the bar. Don't be shy. Even excellent pubs can occasionally serve a bad pint --- it's a live product, don't forget --- but an excellent pub will apologise and replace your pint, and the very best will then test the bad pint and stop selling any more of it.

Should beer be warm or cold?

Ideally real ale should be served at cellar temperature, usually 11-14 degrees Celsius. Real ale may seem warm compared to chilled lagers, but as you'll see at beer festivals where barrels are often covered in wet towels and cooling equipment, we don't want beer too warm or it quickly goes off.

If it's a hot day and you want something cold but good, go for a "real ale lager": that is, a lager that has been made traditionally, rather than the mass-produced heavily-advertised stuff pumped out at iceberg temperatures in so many U.K. pubs. There are U.K. brewers producing real lagers and also good imported lager, like the classic Czech beer Budweiser Budvar. Most British lagers are made too cheaply and too quickly, which is why the same brand of European cold beer tastes better abroad than here. It tastes different because it is different.

Learning to appreciate real ale is just as rewarding as learning to appreciate the differences in any kind of food and drink. While it can be hard to know what is good or bad, it is worth experimenting and taking advice. To ensure you have a good pint, look for a recent CAMRA sticker near a pub entrance.

How is Real Ale made?

The Malt Mill

In a traditional brewery, the first stage takes place at the top of the brewery building, where the barley malt is ground. Most of the malt is ground to flour, but it is blended with coarser grits and the rough husks of the grain. The ground malt is known as "grist", a term that gives us the old English expression "grist to the mill".

The Mash Tun

Traditional ale starts with an infusion mash. The mash tun is like a giant teapot into which the grist is placed with hot pure water, known as the liquor. This thick porridge-like mixture stands in the mash tun for around two hours, as natural enzymes in the malt convert starch into fermentable sugar. The result is known as the wort.

The Coppers

The sweet wort flows to the copper or boiling kettle. The liquid is boiled vigorously for up to two hours and hops are added in three stages: at the start of the boil, halfway through, and again just a few minutes before the boil ends. The natural oils, acids and resins in the hops add bitterness to the wort, and also add some fruity and resin characteristics.

Paraflow

After the copper boil, the hopped wort is pumped through a refrigeration unit, known as a paraflow. Plates containing the boiled liquid are interleaved with plates containing cold water. The paraflow lowers the temperature of the wort prior to the fermentation.

Fermenters

The cool wort is put into fermenting vessels. These are huge open-topped vessels: like giant upended barrels. Yeast is mixed (known in the trade as "pitched") with the wort. For ale brewing, yeast strains are top fermenting: as the yeast transforms the malt sugars into alcohol and carbon dioxide, a thick crust forms on top of the liquid. It takes around two weeks to ensure a full conversion of sugar to alcohol.

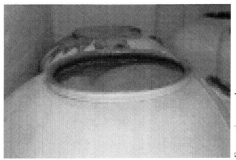

Fermenting vessel

Racking

When fermentation is finished, the "green" beer is left to stand in conditioning tanks for a few days. Then the beer is transferred from the tanks into casks: this is known as cask racking. Additional liquid brewing sugar may be added to encourage a strong second fermentation, and the beer may also be "dry hopped": small amounts of hops are added for extra flavour, bitterness and aroma. Finings or isinglass, made from the swim bladders of fish, are also added. Finings help to clear the beer of yeast, causing it to settle at the bottom of the cask.

Public transport information

Most of the pubs listed in this guide are no more than a few minutes walk from one of the many bus routes serving the Black Country, so it makes good sense to leave the car at home when you go out for a pint or two.

Directions and bus, train and metro information is included for most pubs in the guide. The information was correct at the time of going to press, but you are advised to contact the Traveline hotline on 0870 608 2608 for the latest information. Within the West Midlands, the Traveline facility provides details of all bus services registered within the West Midlands region, which includes the West Midlands County, Herefordshire, Shropshire, Staffordshire, Stoke-on-Trent, Telford, Warwickshire & Worcestershire. The call centre also holds certain information on public transport links to other areas of the country, details of local rail services and selected coach services.

Traveline journey planning web site: www.travelinemidlands. co.uk Telephone: 0870 608 2608.

Centro is the corporate name of the West Midlands Passenger Transport Executive. It is responsible for promoting and developing public transport across the West Midlands metropolitan area.

Centro web site: www.centro.org.uk Telephone: 0121 214 7878.

Travel West Midlands, part of the National Express group, provides a comprehensive network of local bus services in and around the major cities and towns of the West Midlands, including Birmingham, Wolverhampton and Coventry. Timetables and maps also available on-line. Travel WM web site: www.travelwm.co.uk Telephone: 0121 254 7272.

Please Drink Safely.

Metro tram

Black Country Attractions and Nearby Guide Pubs

Bilston

Bilston Craft Gallery and Museum

Mount Pleasant, Bilston, Wolverhampton, WV14 7LU.
Telephone: 01902 552507
Web: www.wolverhamptonart.org.uk
There is a rolling programme of exhibitions, some of which include activities for children. There is a permanent exhibition of eighteenth century locally produced enamels.

Nearby guide pubs

All Bilston pubs.

Brierley Hill

Merry Hill Shopping Centre

Brierley Hill, West Midlands, DY5 1QX.
Telephone: 01384 481141
Web: www.westfield.com/merryhill
One of the largest shopping centres in the U.K.; this was previously the Round Oak Steel Works.

Nearby guide pubs

Abraham Darby, Waterfront, Vine (Bull and Bladder).

Dudley

Black Country Living Museum

Tipton Road, Dudley, DY1 4SQ.
Telephone: 0121 557 99643
Web: www.bclm.co.uk
This is an open-air reconstruction of a Black Country village, as it might have been at the end of the nineteenth century. Ideal for those who find most museums dull and lifeless, this museum shows the skills that made this area the heart of the industrial revolution.

Inside the museum is the Bottle and Glass serving Holden's beers, only a mile from the family brewery.

Nearby guide pubs

Park Inn in Woodsetton.

Black Country Museum

Dudley Tunnel and Caverns Tours

Birmingham New Road, near the junction with Tipton Road, not far from the Black Country Museum.
Admin office: Blowers Green Pump House, Peartree Lane, Dudley.
Telephone: 01384 236275
Web: www.dudleycanaltrust.org.uk/
Next door to the Black Country Museum and accessible from within the museum or the Birmingham New Road, trips are available through the low narrow tunnel. There is the opportunity to try legging: lying on your back on the top of the narrowboat and walking along the ceiling of the low tunnel, to propel the boat. The narrow tunnels open out onto remarkable caverns.

Nearby guide pubs

Park Inn in Woodsetton.

Dudley Zoo

2, The Broadway, Dudley, DY1 4QB.
Telephone: 01384 215314
Web: www.dudleyzoo.org.uk
Ten minutes walk from the Black Country Museum and five minutes from the town centre. The collection includes animals from around the world and a reptile house.
Dudley Castle, once the home to the Earl of Dudley, is in the grounds and can be seen for miles around.

Nearby guide pubs

Old Priory, Full Moon.

Dudley Museum and Art Gallery

St. James's Road, Dudley DY1 1HU.
Telephone: 01384 815575
Web: www.dudley.gov.uk/leisure-and-culture
Well-known for its art and fossils displays. Home to the Brooke Robinson Collection of 19th and 20th century oil paintings, pottery and furniture.

Nearby guide pubs

Full Moon, Old Priory.

Dudley Concert Hall

St. James's Road, Dudley, DY1 1HP.
Telephone: 01384 815577
Web: online.dudley.gov.uk/whatson/townhalls
Formerly the town hall, this is the town's venue for concerts, dances and other entertainment. The Dudley Winter Ales Fayre is held here every November.

Nearby guide pubs

Full Moon, Old Priory.

Royal Brierley Glass Museum

Tipton Road, Dudley, DY1 9SH.
Telephone: 01384 349900
Web: www.royalbrierley.com

Displaced from the factory in Brierley Hill in 2002, this is essentially a shop and glass demonstration area, with educational displays explaining the process. It is conveniently close to the Black Country Museum.

Nearby guide pubs

Park Inn in Woodsetton.

Wren's Nest Nature Reserve

Telephone: 01384 812 785 (warden's office)

Wren's Nest is an area of parkland around a mile to the northeast of Dudley Town Centre and is internationally known as a geology site. The most famous fossil found there is the "The Dudley Bug". The reserve is not only geologically very important but is also home to over 200 species of wild flowers. Wrens Nest was the birthplace of Abraham Darby, the father of the industrial revolution.

Nearby guide pubs

Park Inn, Woodsetton.

Baggeridge Country Park

A463 between Wombourne and Sedgley.

Telephone: 01902 882605

Email: baggeridge.sstaffs@virgin.net

The park is over 152 acres in the valley from Sedgley to Himley Hall and ideal for walking and looking for wildlife. The grounds are open from 9.00am to dusk most days

Himley Hall and Park

Himley Park, Himley, near Dudley, DY3 4DF.

Telephone: 01902 326665

Web: www.dudley.gov.uk/himleyhall

Open all year round, the house often has interesting small exhibitions to look at. The parkland offers good walking, with a large lake to meander around. The oddly distorted Crooked House is in nearby Staffordshire, where coins appear to roll uphill on window ledges in rooms pulled out of shape through subsidence.

Nearby guide pubs

Bulls Head, Five Ways in Lower Gornal.

Halesowen

Leasowes Park

The Leasowes, Leasowes Lane, off Mucklow Hill, Halesowen, B62 8DH.
Telephone: 01384 814642
The Leasowes is a landscape garden of national and international importance and is listed as Grade I by English Heritage. It was laid out as a garden by the poet William Shenstone between 1743 and 1763.

Nearby guide pubs

William Shenstone, Waggon and Horses.

Netherton

Bumble Hole and Warrens Hall Local Nature Reserves

Web: www.nethertondudley.org.uk/bumble.htm
This curiously desolate area was once heavily industrialized and a hub of waterways activity. The Cobbs Engine House, Timbers Gallows Crane and the Blow Cold Bank Colliery Spoil Heap and canal toll island are all that remain. The entrance to the Netherton Tunnel is now a Grade II listed structure, the tunnel being the last tunnel of the canal age to be built. It is wide enough for tow paths: waterproof clothes and a torch are a must for walkers through to the Wolverhampton and Birmingham Canal at Dudley Port.

Cobbs Engine House

Nearby guide pubs

Olde Swan (Ma Pardoe's).

Saltwells Local Nature Reserve

off Coppice Road, Quarry Bank
Telephone: 01384 261572

Saltwells Wood stands at the heart of the nature reserve and, at 40 hectares in size, is the largest woodland in the Borough. In 1992 it became the UK's first reserve under UNESCO's Man and the Biosphere project. Saltwells became part of Lord Dudley's estate in 1785. Wood was in great demand at the time to provide fuel and charcoal for local industry.

Kingswinford

Broadfield House Glass Museum

Compton Drive, Kingswinford, DY6 9NS.
Telephone: 01384 812745.
Web: www.glassmuseum.org.uk

The museum has exhibits that explain how glass is made, blown and cut, with many pieces on display and a studio that ably demonstrate the craftsmanship that made the Stourbridge and Brierley glass well known around the world.

Nearby guide pubs

Park Tavern.

Smethwick

Smethwick Heritage Centre

Victoria Park Lodge, High Street, Smethwick, B66 3NJ.
Telephone: 0121 555 7278
Web: www.smethwick-heritage.co.uk/

This centre, in a converted park keeper's lodge, houses a superb collection of exhibits and artefacts depicting past and present Smethwick life. Glassmaking was the second most important industry, most notably by Chance's, who made all the glass for the Crystal Palace in the mid-nineteenth century. The huge Mitchells and Butlers brewery was built in Cape Hill but closed in 2003.

Nearby guide pubs

Old Chapel.

Smethwick Pump House

Galton Valley Canal Heritage Centre and Smethwick Pump House

Brasshouse Lane Smethwick, B66 1BA.
Telephone 0121 558 8195
Web: www.smethwicktoday.com/environment/canals.htm
Britain's Industrial Revolution grew on the transport provided by the canal system and at the heart of the canal system is the Galton Valley. A visit to the Galton Valley offers visitors a chance to travel back into this exciting era, with fine examples of Industrial architecture from the 18th and 19th Century and a sight of the remarkable pumping station. There are displays showing how canals were constructed.

Nearby guide pubs

Old Chapel.

Stourbridge

Ruskin Glass Centre

Wollaston Road, Amblecote, Stourbridge, DY8 4HF.
Telephone: 01384 399400
Web: www.ruskin-mill.org.uk
The Ruskin Glass Centre is home to a number of craft shops and contemporary and traditional glass makers. The centre also hosts international glass festivals.

Walsall

Jerome K Jerome Birthplace Museum

Belsize House, Bradford Place, Walsall, WS1 1PL.
Telephone: 01922 653116
Web: www.jeromekjerome.com
This museum celebrates the birth of English comic writer Jerome
K. Jerome, the author of such classic whimsical pieces as Three Men
in a Boat and Idle Thoughts of an Idle Fellow.

Nearby guide pubs

Red Lion.

Walsall Leather Museum

Littleton Street West, Walsall, WS2 8EQ.
Telephone: 01922 721153
Web: www.windowsonwalsall.org.uk
The Walsall leather industry was at its peak at the start of the twentieth
century, with over 10,000 people working locally producing saddles,
harnesses and other leather goods. There are still several saddlery
firms in the area, and the trade gives the local Walsall football team
their nickname of The Saddlers.

Nearby guide pubs

Prince, Red Lion, Tap & Spile, Fountain.

Walsall Arboretum

The Arboretum, Walsall, WS1 2AB.
Web: www.walsallarboretum.co.uk
Ten minutes walk from the town centre are over eighty acres of
lakes, parks and gardens. Each September and October, the Walsall
Illuminations take place in the Arboretum, providing some of the
spectacle of Blackpool here in the Midlands.

Nearby guide pubs

Arbor Lights, Fountain.

New Art Gallery

New Art Gallery

Gallery Square, Walsall, WS2 8LG.
Telephone: 01922 654400
Web: www.artatwalsall.org.uk
The gallery opened in 2000 and features many great works of
European art and regular exhibitions.

Nearby guide pubs

Red Lion, Prince.

Walsall Football Club

Bescot Crescent, Walsall, WS1 4SA.
Web: www.saddlers.co.uk

Nearby guide pubs

White Lion, King George V (away supporters).

Wednesbury

Wednesbury Museum and Art Gallery

Holyhead Road, Wednesbury, WS10 7DF.
Telephone: 0121 556 0683
Web: www.sandwell.gov.uk

A recently redecorated Victorian Art Gallery, housing collections which include fine art paintings, applied art, including one of the world's largest collections of Ruskin pottery, and geology. There is a family room dedicated to school and community use, and the education programme features activities such as toy handling, gallery visits, and storytelling linked to the collections.

West Bromwich

Oak House

Oak Road, West Bromwich, B70 8HJ.
Telephone: 0121 553 0759
Web: www.birminghamuk.com/oakhouse.htm

The Oak House offers visitors the chance to experience the Tudor way of life. The house contains a fine selection of oak furniture and features items on loan from the Victoria and Albert Museum. There are tours and special events that take place throughout the year with workshops for school children during the school holidays.

Nearby guide pubs

Billiard Hall, Old Crown, Wheatsheaf.

Sandwell Valley Country Park and Farm

Salters Lane, West Bromwich, B71 4BG.
Telephone: 0121 553 2147
Web: www.sandwellvalley.com
Sandwell Valley has parkland and woodlands, with wildfowl lakes and the remains of an old Benedictine monastery. It also has a farm with a gift shop and refreshments are available. The footpaths include part of the Beacon Way and several nature trails. It is close to junction 1 of the M5.

Nearby guide pubs

Vine.

West Bromwich Albion Football Club

The Hawthorns, Halfords Lane, West Bromwich, B71 4LF.
Web: www.wba.co.uk
West Bromwich Albion has been playing at the Hawthorns for over a hundred years, and this was the first league site to be built in the twentieth century.

Nearby guide pubs

Vine (home supporters).

Willenhall

Willenhall Lock Museum

54, New Road, Willenhall, WV13 2DA.
Telephone: 01902 634542
Web: www.lockmuseum.net
This preserved small Victorian lock-making shop offers demonstrations and displays, explaining the craft and skill of the traditional locksmith. Several rooms have been authentically recreated to convey how the locksmith and his family would have lived two centuries ago.

Nearby guide pubs

Falcon, Malthouse.

Wolverhampton

Art Gallery and Museum

Lichfield Street, Wolverhampton, WV1 1DU.
Telephone: 01902 552040
Web: www.wolverhampton.gov.uk
Built in 1884, the town centre gallery has a fine contemporary art collection, including work by artists as diverse as Gainsborough and Warhol. There are regular exhibitions of international collections.

Nearby guide pubs

All city centre pubs.

Bantock House

Bantock House and Park

Finchfield Road, Wolverhampton, WV3 9LQ.
Telephone: 01902 552195
A grade II listed building that shows the lifestyle of Wolverhampton's Edwardian gentry. The first floor has a display showing the history and development of the city.

Nearby guide pubs

Chindit, Gunmakers, Chestnut Tree.

Civic Hall, Wulfrun Hall

North Street, Wolverhampton, WV1 1RQ.
Telephone: 01902 552121
Web: www.wolvescivic.co.uk
Venues for concerts and also the Wolverhampton Beer Festivals.

Nearby guide pubs

All city centre pubs.

Grand Theatre

Lichfield Street, Wolverhampton, WV1 1DE.
Telephone: 01902 573300
Web: www.grandtheatre.co.uk
A variety of shows, plays and a popular annual pantomime.

Nearby guide pubs:

All city centre pubs.

Graseley Old Hall

Carlton Road, Penn Fields, Wolverhampton, WV3 0LP.
Telephone: 01902 714544
A fifteenth century manor house on one and a half acres of gardens, around one mile from the city centre. Check opening hours.

Lighthouse Centre

The Chubb Buildings, Fryer Street, Wolverhampton, WV1 1HT.
Telephone 01902 716055
Web: www.light-house.co.uk
Two cinema screens and gallery area, with trendy bars in same complex.

Nearby guide pubs

All city centre pubs.

Wolverhampton Wanderers Football Club

Molineux Football Ground, Waterloo Road, Wolverhampton, WV1 4QR.
Telephone: 01902 687052
Web: www.wolves.co.uk
Home to Wolverhampton Wanderers, the ground is 10 minutes walk from the city centre and from the railway station.

Nearby guide pubs

Feathers (home supporters), Stile (home supporters).

Race Course

Dunstall Park, Wolverhampton, WV6 0PE.
Telephone: 0870 220 2442
Web: www.wolverhampton-racecourse.co.uk
Racing during the day and evening and regular camera and computer fairs.

Speedway and Greyhound Racing

Ladbroke Stadium, Sutherland Avenue, Monmore Green, Wolverhampton, WV2 2JJ.
Web: www.wolverhampton-speedway.com
Web: www.monmoredogs.co.uk

Nearby guide pubs

Red Lion.

Wightwick Manor

Wightwick Bank, Compton, Wolverhampton, WV6 8EE.
Telephone: 01922 761108
Web: www.nationaltrust.org.uk
This Victorian mansion contains some of the finest examples of the work of William Morris and other artists influenced by the Pre-Raphaelites. Morris was a prolific designer of wallpapers and fabrics.

Nearby guide pubs

Fieldhouse.

Wightwick Manor

Wordsley

Red House Cone Glassworks Experience

Red House Glassworks, Wordsley, Stourbridge, DY8 4AA.
Telephone: 01384 828282
Web: www.stourbridge.com/htm/glass.htm
Web: www.redhousecone.co.uk
The last remaining glass cone, this is now a demonstration area for glass making and a chance to walk around a piece of history. Modern glassmakers work in studios around the cone and there are plenty of styles of glass to buy.

Nearby guide pubs
Maverick in Amblecote.

Red House glass cone

Tourism Offices

Black Country Tourism

Black Country House, Rounds Green Road, Oldbury, B69 2DG.
Email: info@blackcountrytourism.co.uk
Web: www.blackcountrytourism.co.uk

Dudley

259, Castle Street, Dudley, DY1 1LQ.
Telephone: 01384 812830 / 01384 812345
Email: tourism@dudley.gov.uk

Walsall

St. Paul's Bus Station, St. Paul's Street, Walsall, WS1 1NR.
Telephone: 01922 625540
Email: walsalltt&i@travelwm.co.uk
Web: www.walsall.gov.uk/leisure/tourism

Wolverhampton

18, Queen Square, Wolverhampton, WV1 1TQ.
Telephone: 01902 556110
Email: wolverhampton.tic@dial.pipex.com
Web: www.wolverhampton.tic.dial.pipex.com

CAMRA's statement of aims

CAMRA's mission is to act as the champion of the consumer in relation to the UK and European drinks industry.

It aims to

• Maintain consumer rights

• Promote quality, choice and value for money

• Support the public house as a focus. of community life

• Campaign for greater appreciation of traditional beers, ciders and perries as part of national heritage and culture

CAMRA exists to promote and preserve full flavoured and distinctive beers and decent pubs.

Bilston

Bilston can be traced back to at least 994. In the 13th century Henry III granted lands to Walter De Bilston for his services in the battle of Evesham. By 1315 coal and iron was being mined, and Bilston's famed enamel trade can be traced back to at least 1760. John Wilkinson set up his smelting works in 1757 which led to its growth as a industrial area.

In 1824 Bilston was granted its charter and rapidly grew with houses and pubs being built quickly and poorly. In 1831 many of its citizens succumbed to a cholera outbreak which spread quickly due to the poor sanitary conditions. The 1850's saw much redevelopment which included an enormous number of pubs to satisfy the thirsts of its industrial workers: on some streets every other building was a public house.

Not many of those old pubs survived the various stages of redevelopment of the town. The oldest surviving pub is the Greyhound & Punchbowl High Street which dates back to the 16th century. It was originally the Manor House for nearby Stowheath but by 1818 it was being used as a pub. Major structural rebuilding was done in the 1920's and 1930's which saved it from demolition. One room still retains its original hearth, grate, wooden panels and ornate ceiling.

Bilston became part of Wolverhampton in 1966 and it is slowly recovering from the loss of much of its heavy industry.

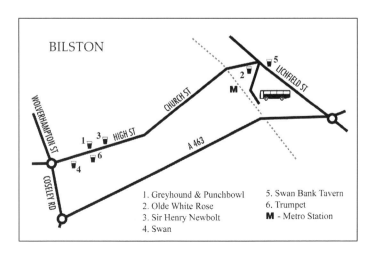

BILSTON

1. Greyhound & Punchbowl
2. Olde White Rose
3. Sir Henry Newbolt
4. Swan
5. Swan Bank Tavern
6. Trumpet
M - Metro Station

Bilston

Greyhound & Punchbowl

51 High Street, WV14 0ED

🕐 12:00-23:00 Mon-Sat; 12:00-22:30 Sun

☎ 07708 827754

Banks's Original; Greene King Abbot Ale; guest beer

Built in the 16th century, this grade II* listed building was the former Bilston manor house. By 1934, in danger of collapsing, the building was awaiting demolition; however its importance was recognised and after major restoration, it re-opened as a public house in 1936. Although opened out, the room on the left features an ornate ceiling, wooden panelling and a superb hearth with its real fire. Visit and enjoy.

🏨◖⊖(Bilston Central)

Olde White Rose

20 Lichfield Street, WV14 0AG

🕐 12:00-23:00 Mon-Thu; 12:00-23:30 Fri-Sat; 12:00-22:30 Sun

☎ (01902) 498339

Beer range varies

A long narrow pub with a listed frontage. It offers up to 12 real ales, a wide variety of foreign beers, plus Westons cider and perry. Live music is held in the bierkeller on Thur eve. In addition to the menu served 12-9, a carvery is offered lunchtime and evening (12-5 Sun). Handy for bus and metro stations.

❀◖ ♿♣⊖(Bilston Central)

Sir Henry Newbolt

45-47 High Street, WV14 0EP

🕐 09:00-00:00 Sun-Thu; 09:00-01:00 Fri-Sat

☎ (01902) 404636

Greene King Abbot Ale; Marston's Burton Bitter; guest beers

A typical Wetherspoon's conversion of an old cinema building which opened in 2000. Its frontage, designed to blend in with other nearby buildings, means you can easily walk past without realising. Its name refers to a famous Bilston poet.

Q◖♣⊖(Bilston Central)

Swan

84 High Street, WV14 0HH

🕐 12:00-23:00 Mon-Sat; 12:00-22:30 Sun

☎ (01902) 353959

Banks's Original, Bitter

A small Banks's pub situated at the top of High Street. It was built over a century ago as a direct replacement for Swan at Swanbank, now the site of Barclays Bank. It originally had two rooms, but has now been opened out with a central bar which serves its varied customers.

❀◖P⊖(Bilston Central)

Swan Bank Tavern

Swanbank, Lichfield Street, WV14 0AG

🕐 11:00-23:00 Mon-Sat; 12:00-15:00, 19:00-22:30 Sun

☎ (01902) 495790

Banks's Original, Bitter

This basic Banks's pub has a bar and lounge and is named after the location in which it stands. For years it was known by its local customers as the (Blazing) Stump. Local folklore tells that many years ago a drunken customer had set fire to the landlord's wooden leg. Wolverhampton to Birmingham bus 79 stops nearby.

❀⇦⊖ (Bilston Central)

Trumpet

58 High Street, WV14 0EP

🕐 11:00-15:00, 19:30-23:00 Mon-Sat; 12:00-15:00, 19:30-22:30 Sun

☎ (01902) 493723

Holden's Mild, Bitter, Golden Glow, Special; guest beer

With its mixture of Holden's beers and nightly jazz sessions, it attracts a very mixed clientele. Originally called the Royal Exchange prior to adopting its current name, which reflects its music links. This small one roomed pub can get very crowded some evenings.

❀⊖ (Bilston Central)

Black Country Food

Frumity

One of the most famous Black Country dishes was Frumity or Frumenty. It was the custom at harvest time for women and girls to pick up scattered ears of corn, to be made into miniature sheaves. These would be hung in the rafters until Mothering Sunday, when they are taken down and the grains soaked for several hours.

The grains were then put into a stew-pot and stewed until soft. With the addition of milk, sugar or treacle, the frumity would be something that everyone consumed at the Sunday dinner.

Grey Peas and Bacon

Locally pronounced "grey pays 'n' bacon", this inexpensive dish is still popular and available in some of the local pubs. It is made by the long boiling of grey peas, sometimes called pigeon peas, with the addition of bacon in the later stages of boiling.

A poem extolling the virtues of this tasty concoction reads:
Peas and bacon in a pot
Stewed till they be tender got;
Served up in a trencher wide
To match the room in your inside.

Faggots and Peas

This celebrated Black Country dish, pronounced locally "faggits and pays", consists of:
One and a half pounds of Pig's fry or one pound belly pork and half pound bacon
Two medium size onions
One cup of breadcrumbs
One tablespoon dried sage
Salt and pepper to season
One tablespoon of plain flour mixed with water to thicken the gravy

Wash the fry. Mince or chop the meat and onions and mix well with the breadcrumbs, seasoning and sage. Divide into eight portions and shape into balls. Bake for around three hours in a low oven (around 150 degrees C), basting frequently until well browned.
Serve with mushy peas: dried peas soaked overnight, then steamed or slowly boiled until the peas are so soft that they merge.

Groaty Dick

Resisting the temptation to include a witticism that might be considered inappropriate in this enlightened time, here instead is the recipe for this local dish.
A half pound of groats
One and a half pounds of shin beef
One pound of sliced leeks
Two medium size sliced onions
Salt and pepper to taste

Combine the ingredients and place in a covered container bowl or similar. Place in a pan of hot water and boil slowly for three hours or longer. Serve with boiled potatoes and fresh crusty bread.

Groats are an oats cereal. The oats are kiln-dried and stored for a day when the husks can be removed. The resulting groats can be ground to produce oatmeal.

Bread Pudding

Two pounds of stale bread
Half a pound of shredded suet
One pound of brown or granulated sugar
One pound of mixed dried fruit
Three eggs
Two ounces of butter or margarine
Spices such as cinnamon or nutmeg to taste

Soak the bread well for thirty minutes in water, then drain and squeeze out the excess moisture.

Flake the bread then add the remaining ingredients. Mix well and spread evenly in a greased baking tin. Add a few curls of butter and bake in a moderate oven for around two hours or until nicely browned.

Stuffed Pigs Ears

Soak the pig ears in water for about five hours.

Meanwhile, make a filling of breadcrumbs, suet, parsley, thyme, pepper and beaten eggs.

The stuffing is packed into the soaked ears, which are then sealed with a thread and lightly fried.

The ears are then poached gently in stock for an hour or so, when they can be served with a sauce made from the stock.

The editor of this beer guide confesses to having neither cooked nor tasted this alleged delicacy. While he would be interested in receiving comments and accurate ingredient measurements, samples are unnecessary.

Blackheath

Prior to the mid-19th century, Blackheath, or Bleak Heath as it was more commonly known, was little more than the meeting point of several roads in an area of heath land surrounded by a few scattered farms. Expansion of coal and ironstone mining and the development of brick making and other industries resulted in rapid growth of the population. Local agricultural workers became employed in these industries and additional labour was attracted from further afield. Housing and associated facilities expanded to accommodate the increased workforce. Blackheath evolved a shopping centre and its character, with streets of small shops, has altered remarkably little for over a century. Today Blackheath is largely a residential area for commuters.

Blackheath

Bell and Bear

71 Gorsty Hill Road, B65 0HA
On A4099 Blackheath to Halesowen road

☉ 11:30-23:00 Mon-Fri; 11:00-23:00 Sat; 11:30-22:30 Sun

☎ (0121) 561 2196

Taylor Landlord, guest beers

Fine 400 year-old listed pub with a small area set aside for non-smokers. The pub is noted for its extensive patio and garden areas that afford splendid views over the Black Country and beyond. Food available all day. Popular pub quizzes on Thursday and Sunday evenings.

🍺◖P☺

Britannia

124 Halesowen Street, B65 0ES
In Blackheath town centre, opp. Sainsbury's

☉ 09:00-00:00 Sun-Thu, 09:00-01:00 Fri-Sat

☎ (0121) 559 0010

www.jdwetherspoon.co.uk

Beer range varies

The ales in this JDW free house are better served than some of their nearby outlets, making this Wetherspoons worth popping into. Unusually for the pubco, the Britannia has always been a pub and is not converted from a shop or office. This one ticks most of the boxes, having a car park, well kept garden, no smoking area and a dining area serving the usual JDW menu. Close to Rowley Regis railway station and all buses that stop in Blackheath.

🍺◖♿♥P☺≋

Knights Quest

126 High Street, B65 0EE

⏰ 11:00-00:00 Sun-Thu; 11:00-02:00 Fri-Sat

☎ (0121) 561 5599

Banks's Original, Bitter; guest beer

Previously the George & Dragon, this pub has played a part in Blackheath's history over the past two centuries. It was originally the site of a farmhouse that gradually lost its land to the mining industry. This led to its establishment as a drinking house in the 1830s. The present building, which dates to the 1930s, has a large lounge and smaller bar. There are benches outside in the large car park. Frequent live entertainment. Carvery and pub meals served 12-3, 6-9 Mon-Sat; 12-4 Sun. Five minutes walk from Blackheath centre which is served by buses from Dudley, Halesowen, Oldbury, Walsall, West Bromwich, and Birmingham.

🕸🍴🛋♣P

Lighthouse

153 Coombs Road, B62 8AF

On A4099 towards Blackheath

⏰ 12:00-23:00 Mon-Thu; 11:00-00:00 Fri-Sat; 11:00-22:30 Sun

☎ (0121) 602 1620 www.sabrain.com

Enville Ale; Holden's Golden Glow; Ever changing SA Brains seasonal / guest

An uphill walk from Old Hill station, this outpost of Welsh brewer and pubco SA Brains has recently lost the landmark lighthouse painting on the outside as a result of a smart modern refurb. There is now disabled access to the whole pub which has plush sofas and low tables in the bar area, a no smoking dining area and a separate seating area where regular events are held. The three real ales are well kept and are served at the cooler end of the real ale temperature spectrum which is very refreshing for summer drinkers.

🕸🍴♿P⊗≷(Old Hill)

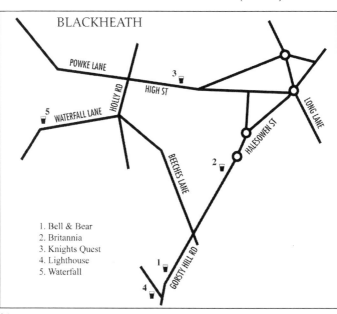

BLACKHEATH

1. Bell & Bear
2. Britannia
3. Knights Quest
4. Lighthouse
5. Waterfall

Waterfall

Waterfall Lane, Old Hill, B64 6RG

Just off main Blackheath to Old Hill road.

🕐 12:00-14:00, 17:00-23:00 Mon-Thu; 12:00-00:00 Fri-Sat; 12:00-22:30 Sun

☎ (0121) 561 3499

www.holdensbrewery.co.uk

Holden's Mild, Bitter, Golden Glow, Special; guest beers

A short uphill walk from Old Hill railway station, this pub is perched on the steep and aptly named Waterfall Lane. It's officially in Cradley Heath, but is nearer to Blackheath town centre. It was an early beacon for local real ale lovers in the 1980's and is now owned by Holden's brewery, though the pub still has a free house feel, due to the wide range of guest ales. A back-to-front pub with the lounge in the front and the bar with a darts board at the back. Because of its elevated position, the outdoor patio area affords distant views to the West in the summer.

🏰🌞🍴🚲♣P⇌(Old Hill)

THE WAZZIN WASH

yoe stond theer thinking "wheer con ah goo?"
the Black Country's the plairce for a bostin brew
wheer yoe con meet sum decent folk
wet ya wazzin un tell a joke;
join the campaign for real ale clubs
they'm the best yoe'll meet for pints in pubs
ther's pub crawls, brewery trips an wikends away
an the booze they drink, flows all day
protectin' real ale for many a year
the fun they 'ave supping a beer
munthly meetings to air ya views
spakin abaht the local pub news
lots of indipendunt brews ter tairst
un every one wull quench ya thirst
so cum un join us - it's no fuss
or yoe'l end up drinkin lager… now that **is** wuss
wunce a wazzin wash of malt n' hops is sunk
ther's no betta way of gooin um than drunk

by Peter Hill

Bloxwich

The Wyrley & Essington canal brought about the expansion of Bloxwich. Small cottage industries existed making various metal parts such as nails, needles, saddle blades, awls, bits and tacks. The "King of Showmen" Pat Collins lived in Bloxwich for many years in Lime Tree House, now demolished.

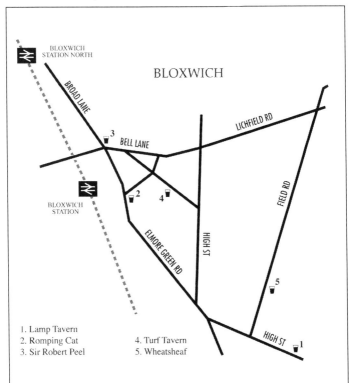

1. Lamp Tavern
2. Romping Cat
3. Sir Robert Peel
4. Turf Tavern
5. Wheatsheaf

Local CAMRA contact details

To contact your local CAMRA branch, visit their website:

Dudley - www.dudleycamra.org.uk

Stourbridge - www.stourbridge-camra.co.uk

Wolverhampton - wolverhamptoncamra.org.uk

or the national website - www.camra.org.uk

Bloxwich

Beacon Way

Stoney Lane, WS3 3DW

🕐 12:00-23:00 Mon-Sat; 12:00-22:30 Sun

☎ (01922) 694555

Beer range varies

Recently refurbished to provide a large open plan modern lounge area with widescreen TV facilities and a separate restaurant area. This pub has a strict over 21 rule and smart dress code.

❀&P

Lamp Tavern

34 High Street, WS3 2DA

🕐 10:00-02:00 Mon-Sat; 12:00-22:30 Sun

☎ (01922) 479681

Holden's Mild, Bitter, seasonal beers

This cosy one roomed pub on the outskirts of Bloxwich town centre, was created out of former farm buildings and stables. It retains much olde-worlde charm This strong community pub features a separate restaurant attached to the pub.

🏚Q❀&P

Romping Cat

96-97 Elmore Green Road, WS3 2HF

🕐 14:00-23:00 Mon-Sat; 12:00-15:00, 19:00-22:30 Sun

☎ (01922) 475041

Banks's Original, Bitter; guest beer

Now Grade II listed, the pub has recently been tastefully refurbished. This is a fine example of a late Victorian three roomed corner pub and is included in CAMRAs national inventory of pub interiors. With its attractive brickwork and round arched windows on the

ground floor it provides a focal point for the local community.

🏚Q❀⊞♣☀≈

Sir Robert Peel

104 Bell Lane, WS3 2JS

🕐 12:00-23:00 Mon-Sun

☎ (01922) 470921

Beer range varies

Situated on the edge of Bloxwich town centre, this large corner pub boasts a separate restaurant and function room. The traditional two roomed pub has a separate bar and rear beer garden.

❀◖⊞♣P

Turf Tavern

13 Wolverhampton Road, WS3 2EZ

🕐 12:00-15:00, 19:00-23:00 Mon-Sat; 12:00-15:00, 19:00-22:30 Sun

☎ (01922) 407743

Batham's Best Bitter; Titanic Mild; guest beers

Known locally as Tinky's, this grade II listed, three roomed unspoilt gem has been in the same family for 130 years. Unusual seating in the bar and smoke room, plus William Morris style wallpaper and a tiled floor add to the immense character of this terraced pub.

Q❀⊗≈

Wheatsheaf

35 The Pinfold, WS3 3JL

🕐 11:00-23:00 Mon-Sat; 12:00-22:30 Sun

☎ (01922) 449292

Beer range varies

A friendly out of town local with a traditional style bar, cosy snug and separate restaurant. Within walking distance of town centre.

🏚Q❀⊞♣

Bradley

Bradley is a small enclave to the south of Bilston town centre and to the east of Coseley. Although now fully a part of Bilston, the older locals still proudly declare they are from Bradley not Bilston. The decline of the steel and other heavy industries has hit the area hard. Nearly half the pubs in this area have closed in the last five years.

Bradley

Great Western

1 Ash Street, WV14 8UP

🕒 16:00-23:00 Mon-Thu; 12:00-23:00 Fri-Sat; 12:00-22:30 Sun

☎ (01902) 494173

Banks's Original, Bitter

Small intimate pub built around 1860. Crib and darts are played in the bar, the rear lounge occasionally hosts live entertainment. The railway line that the pub's name refers to closed in the 1960's.

🍺♣

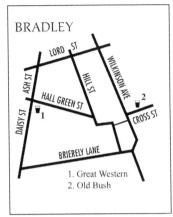

Old Bush

15 Cross Street, WV14 8DL

1/2 mile along Bradley Lane from Metro station

🕒 12:00-15:30, 18:00-23:00 Mon-Thu; 12:00-23:00 Fri-Sat; 12:00-22:30 Sun

☎ (01902) 492115

Banks's Original, Bitter

Small community pub built around 1860 as a beer house. It consists of two small rooms, a bar with a dart board at the front, and a cosy lounge along the corridor at the back. Buses 401, 525 & 531 stop in Wilkinson Avenue; bus 530 stops in Stirling Road (off Bradley Lane).

Q🍺♣⊖(Bradley Lane)

Mild: A Tasty, Distinctive Ale

Cask conditioned Mild has become a rarity in a lot of pubs, even in traditional Mild drinking areas such as the West Midlands. This is a great pity because Mild is a distinctive and tasty beer. Mild is one of the oldest beer styles in the country.

So what is Mild? It is a beer which has tastes and textures all its own. Basically it is a beer that is hopped less than bitter. The colour of dark Milds, such as Greene King XX Mild, comes from the use of darker malts and/or roasted barley that are used to compensate for the loss of Hop character. "Chocolate", "fruity", "nutty" and "burnt" are all tastes to be found in various Milds. However, not all Milds are Dark. Yorkshire-brewed Timothy Taylor's Golden Best and Olde Swan Original, brewed in Netherton, are examples of light-coloured Milds and Banks's Original, brewed in Wolverhampton, is amber in colour.

Milds today tend to have a strength of between 3% and 3.5% ABV, with some notable exceptions. Mild wasn't always weaker than bitter: in the latter half of the 19th Century, Milds were brewed to about the same strength as bitters which were around 6% to 7% ABV. However, due to malt rationing in the First World War, coupled with a drive by the temperance movement, the strengths were reduced. Today there are some strong Milds such as Sarah Hughes Dark Ruby Mild at 6% which is brewed to an original early 20th century recipe.

The keg lager boom has seen Mild's share of the market reduce significantly but fortunately all is far from lost. The last few years have seen Mild make a very small, but significant recovery, though unfortunately not to the mass market. A Mild (Moorhouses Black Cat) also won Champion Beer of Britain at the Great British Beer Festival in 2000.

The Campaign for Real Ale can also claim a hand in the fortunes of Mild. The old Mild Task Group kept the flag flying for years , and now renamed and revamped as the Light and Dark Supporters (and championing other threatened styles such as Stouts, Porters and Old Ales), continues to go MAD ABOUT MILD !!

As the weather forecast would have it, 'The Outlook is Mild'. Make sure you try some soon.

Brierley Hill

Until around 1750, Brierley Hill was just that – 'a hill covered with briars' plus a few farms. In the heart of the Black Country, these hills were soon covered with small settlements interspersed among mines and their spoil heaps, coke ovens, blast furnaces and brick, iron and glass works. This gave rise to the ditty:

> When Satan stood on Brierley Hill
>
> And far round it gazed
>
> He said "I never more shall feel
>
> At Hell's fierce flames amazed"

The metal working industries, most notably the famous Round Oak Steelworks, are now gone but the town centre remains a busy, bustling place. Downhill from the high street is the massive modern Merry Hill Shopping Centre with around 250 stores. The Dudley No 1 canal has been redeveloped in this area to complement the Waterfront office complex, whilst the impressive Delph Locks retain the traditional character of the canal era.

On the Stourbridge Canal at Wordsley stands the Red House Glass Cone. Once a familiar sight in the district, this is the only glass cone left locally and one of only four surviving in the whole of the UK.

Brierley Hill: Brockmoor

Rose & Crown

161 Bank Street, DY5 3DD
B4179, off Brierley Hill High Street
🕐 12:00-14:00, 18:00-23:00 Mon-Thu; 12:00-16:00, 18:00-23:00 Fri-Sat; 12:00-15:00, 19:00-22:30 Sun
☎ (01384) 77825
Holden's Mild, Bitter, Special, seasonal beers; guest beer
Small traditional bar and lounge plus non-smoking conservatory extension. Good value pub food served 12-2 and 6-8 Mon-Sat. Outdoor drinking area to the side of the pub. Buses from Halesowen/Old Hill/Cradley Heath/Merry Hill shopping centre: 138 (evenings only); from Dudley/Merry Hill shopping centre: 222; from Dudley/Stourbridge: 246, 311, 312, 313 to Brierley Hill High Street then a 5 minute walk.

🌼🍴🔌♣P🚭

Brierley Hill: Delph

Vine (Bull & Bladder)

10 Delph Road, DY5 2TN
B4172
🕐 12:00-23:00 Mon-Sat; 12:00-22:30 Sun
☎ (01384) 78293
Batham's Mild, Best Bitter, XXX (winter)
Home of Batham's brewery. "Blessings of your heart, you brew good ale" (Shakespeare - Two Gentlemen of Verona) is proclaimed across the frontage of this famous Black Country pub, welcoming visitors from

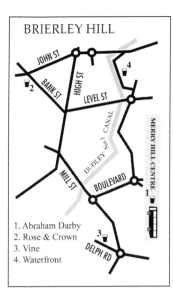

BRIERLEY HILL

1. Abraham Darby
2. Rose & Crown
3. Vine
4. Waterfront

far and near. There are various rooms off a long central corridor and a patio at the rear. Good value hot and cold food is served weekday lunchtimes. Bar snacks available at other times. Buses from Halesowen/Old Hill/Cradley Heath/Merry Hill shopping centre: 139, 138 (evenings only) to Mill Street then a short walk down Delph Road; from Dudley/Stourbridge: 246, 311, 312, 313 to Brierley Hill High Street then a 15 minute walk.

Q❄️🐕🏵️◐🪑♣P

Brierley Hill: Merry Hill Centre
Abraham Darby
Merry Hill Centre, DY5 1QX
Off A4100/A4036
🕐 08:00-00:00 Mon-Thu; 08:00-01:00 Fri-Sat; 09:00-00:00 Sun
☎ (01384) 472850
Enville Ale; Greene King Abbot Ale; Marston's Burton Bitter, Pedigree; guest beers

Modern Wetherspoon pub on the outside of the Merry Hill Shopping centre (exit by Virgin Megastore). For those who prefer to avoid the retail experience, it is conveniently situated just round the corner from the bus station. With a large drinking pavement in front of the building, covered by awning, it has a continental feel. Inside is totally non-smoking. Sound-free TV screen for news and sport. Food served until 11pm.

Q🏵️◐🍎🏵️🚫

Brierley Hill: Waterfront
Waterfront Inn
6-7 The Waterfront, Level Street, DY5 1XE
Between A461 and A4036
🕐 09:00-00:00 Sun-Thu; 09:00-02:00 Fri-Sat
☎ (01384) 262096
Enville Ale; Greene King Abbot Ale; Marston's Burton Bitter, Pedigree; guest beers

Welcoming Wetherspoon's pub in the Waterfront complex. The offices behind provide the lunchtime trade. In the evenings, the proximity to other bars and clubs means it can get very busy. Food is served until 11pm. The pub overlooks the Dudley No 1 canal (with moorings nearby) and has seating on the front pavement from where the scenery can be admired. The famous Delph locks can be reached by a canalside stroll. Buses from Dudley: 276 (daytime only) to Waterfront Way then a 5 minute walk; from Dudley/Stourbridge: 246, 311, 312, 313 to Dudley Road then a 5 minute walk.

Q🏵️◐🍎🏵️🚫

Brownhills

In Brownhills and nearby Walsall Wood it was coal mining on which the town was built. Chasewater was built in 1799, as a reservoir to feed the growing canal network: this is now a water activity centre. The Chasewater Light Railway runs trains around the west and north sides every Sunday, Saturdays from July to September, plus Bank Holiday Mondays.

Brownhills

Anchor

1 Chester Road, WS8 6DP

☉ 11:00-23:00 Mon-Sat; 12:00-22:30 Sun

☎ (01543) 360219

Banks's Original, Bitter

Typical newish W&D pub. One large open plan room with two distinct no smoking areas. Food served all day every day. Big screen TV caters for fans of all major sporting events. Outside drinking area at front of pub.

❀◗&♣P⊗

New Hussey Arms

Chester Road, WS8 7JP

☉ 11:30-23:00 Mon-Sat; 12:00-22:30 Sun

☎ (01543) 370700

Beer range varies

Recently refurbished pub that now includes a restaurant "The Spaghetti Factory" specialising in Italian food. Pub area is comfortably decorated with two regularly changing guest beers available. Food is served 12-2.30 5.30-9.45 Mon-Fri, 12-9.45 Sat and 12-8.30 Sun.

❀◗&P

Royal Oak

68 Chester Road, WS8 6DU

On A452

☉ 12:00-15:00, 18:00-23:00 Mon-Fri; 12:00-15:30, 18:00-23:00 Sat; 12:00-15:30, 19:00-22:30 Sun

☎ (01543) 452089

www.theroyaloakpub.co.uk

Banks's Original; Caledonian Deuchars IPA; Greene King Abbot Ale; Taylor Landlord; Tetley Bitter; guest beers

Locally known as The Middle Oak. A no smoking dining area is found at the rear of the large lounge. The public bar boasts traditional pub games and an impressive array of handpumps. Alongside the range of regular beers there are up to two changing guest beers available.

⋈❀◗🍴♣P⊗

THEER GUZ ANUTHA ONE

Ay it a shairm the way ah pubs am destroyed?
It meks me mad and really annoyed;
Ther's classic boozers still aht theer,
But gooin quickly every 'ear.

Ther ay a wik withaht one down,
Who cares? I say this with a frown;
An empty spairce lies all ararnd
Nuthin theer, there ay a sarnd.

They'm plairces wheer all folk meet
To have a chat, a loff, a friendly greet:
Full of life and atmosphere,
But brewers say they doe need one round 'ere.

Wheer a mighty row of pubs wunce stood
Is deserted land, just med of mud;
The streets at night lie jed and still,
Vandals and muggers arrive at will.

Pubs am moower than just drinking beer:
Yoe learn about the world aht theer;
The last of England, it's bin said,
Is when the last pub lies down jed.

So everyone think of ah tradition,
Or yoe'll all end up watchin just television;
Doe shrug ya shoulders, when a pub as gone,
And blart, oh well, theer guz anutha one.

By Peter Hill

Coseley

Coseley is a widespread area once known officially as 'Lower Sedgley'. Collieries and ironworks abounded, particularly along the route of the canal. In the early 19th century Thomas Telford rerouted parts of the Birmingham to Wolverhampton Main Line canal to take a more direct course. The 360 yard long Coseley tunnel reduced the line by several miles. The area remains a mixture of industrial and residential. There is a small shopping centre at Roseville, just off the main Birmingham to Wolverhampton road (A4123) which bisected Coseley in the late 1920s.

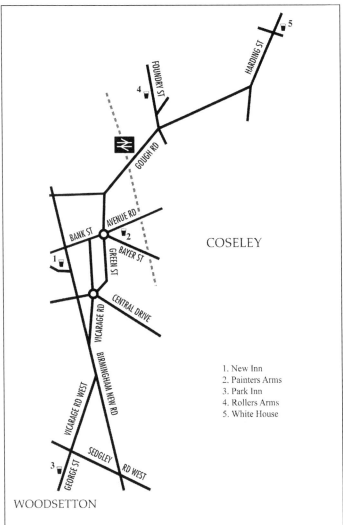

COSELEY

1. New Inn
2. Painters Arms
3. Park Inn
4. Rollers Arms
5. White House

WOODSETTON

Coseley

Painters Arms

33 Avenue Road, WV14 9DJ
off A4123

☼ 11:00-23:00 Mon-Sat; 12:00-22:30 Sun

☎ (01902) 883095

Holden's Mild, Bitter, Special, seasonal beers

Acquired by Holden's in 1928 when the founding Holden, Edwin Alfred became the licensee. This is a lively, Black Country local with a long L-shaped bar running the length of the pub. Tile-floored and bar-like at the front, plusher and lounge-like at the back. There is also a tiny snug. Small outdoor patio overlooking car park. Cobs served. Buses from Dudley/ Wolverhampton: 125, 126 to Birmingham New Road then a 5 minute walk. 5 minute walk from Coseley railway station.

🏚️●♣P🚽≠(Coseley)

Rollers Arms

59 Foundry Street, WV14 8XW
Off B4483

☼ 12:00-23:00 Mon-Sat; 12:00-18:00, 19:00-22:30 Sun

☎ (01902) 497581

Banks's Original, Bitter

Friendly back-street local converted from 4 cottages dating back to the 16th century. The cellar is reputedly haunted by two nuns. The main, tile-floored, bar is popular for traditional pub games. There is also a cosy lounge and a small garden. Occasional live music Saturday nights. Buses from Dudley/Wolverhampton: 125,126 to Birmingham New Road and a 10 minute walk. Close to Coseley railway station.

●♣P🚽≠(Coseley)

Coseley: Daisy Bank

White House

1 Daisy Street, WV14 8QQ
B4163

☼ 12:00-15:00, 18:00-23:00 Mon-Sat; 12:00-15:00, 19:00-22:30 Sun

☎ (01902) 402703

Everards Mild, Beacon, Tiger, Old Original; guest beer

Welcoming family-run free house dominating a suburban crossroads. Behind the imposing exterior the pub has 2 cosy rooms: a bar with pub games and TV and a lounge with a large collection of pottery cats. Good value food is served at lunchtimes and bar snacks in the evenings until 7.30 (not Sun). Buses from Dudley/ Wolverhampton: 525 (daytime only), 544. 15 minute walk from Coseley railway station. 20 minute walk from Loxdale metro stop.

🏚️●(🚽♣≠(Coseley)

Coseley: Hurst Hill

Gate Hangs Well

Hurst Road, WV14 9EU
On A463 between Birmingham New Rd & Sedgley

☼ 12:00-00:00 Mon-Sat; 12:00-22:30 Sun

☎ (01902) 884868

Banks's Bitter, Hanson's Mild

Standard Banks's Pub with a smart lounge and a bar which occasionally hosts live music and discos, which can get noisy. It is a local meeting place where everyone knows each other: the last three tenants still come in to drink. Buses 545 & 546 stop nearby.

Q●🚽♿♣P🚽

New Inn

35 Ward Street, Coseley, WV14 9LQ
A4123

🕐 16:00-23:00 Mon-Fri; 12:00-23:00
Sat; 12:00-22:30 Sun

☎ (01902) 676777

Holden's Mild, Bitter, seasonal beers
Although the front entrance of
the pub is tucked away on peaceful
Ward Street, its rear entrance
and car park are accessed from
Birmingham New Road. Inside is
one large room but separated into
cosy areas. Small outdoor patio
overlooking car park. Meals served
6-8 Tue-Fri. Thatchers cider is sold
in summer. Buses from Dudley/
Wolverhampton: 125, 126. 15
minute walk from Coseley railway
station.

🎪🌸🌙⛄♣🍂P⊗🚆(Coseley)

Brewing in the Boroughs of Dudley and Sandwell

In the 1860's with no affordable transport for the working class, people tended to spend their whole life in the same town or village. This the reason for the many different accents that abound in this area of the Black Country. With most of the work manual and with the lack of safe clean drinking water, there was a need to quench thirsts. This led to the many Beerhouses in the area who brewed their own beer for their customers. Some of those carried on for some time while others stopped brewing and relied on beer from the emerging retail brewers. A few of those emerging brewers were to survive only a short time and others grew often by acquiring their competitors.

The following is a snapshot of some of them.

Daniel Batham & Son, Delph Brewery, Delph Road, Brierley Hill:

A small brewery established in 1877. It has remained in the same family throughout. In 1905 the brewery at the Vine Inn (Bull & Bladder) was established and still carries on producing its excellent ales for its tied houses and the free trade.

Holden's Brewery, George Street, Woodsetton, Dudley:

This family run brewery was established in the 1920s as a home brew house by Edwin and Lucy Holden when they took over the Park Inn. It has expanded over the years and still supplies its excellent ales to both its tied pubs and the free trade.

Sarah Hughes Brewery, Bilston Street, Sedgley:

The brewery was established behind the Beacon Hotel in 1921 and started to brew the beer now known as Dark Ruby. It ceased brewing in 1957 and the brewery laid idle for 30 years. In 1987 grandson John Hughes reopened the brewery using the original recipe for Dark Ruby. It supplies beers to the Beacon Hotel and the free trade.

Ma Pardoes (Olde Swan) Brewery, Halesowen Road, Netherton, Dudley:

Both the pub and the brewery were built in 1863 and it was run for many years by its matriarch Ma Pardoe hence its more well known name. It carried on brewing until 1988 when the brewery closed, the pub however remained open. Brewing restarted in 2001 primarily to supply the pub again, some beers are supplied to other outlets.

Julia Hanson, High Street, Dudley:

Established 1847 in Priory Street, by 1895 they were a registered company and had built their new brewery in High Street. Expansion continued quickly and by 1919 they had acquired over 100 pubs. In 1934 they expanded further by buying Smith & Williams Town Brewery, Round Oak and their 50 pubs. However in 1943 they were taken over by Wolverhampton & Dudley Breweries. Brewing carried on at the site until 1991 when it ceased and the site was sold for redevelopment.

Bert & Don Millard, Little Model Brewery, Stafford Street, Dudley:

In 1870 Thomas Millard purchased the Jolly Collier Home Brew House and renamed it the Gypsies Tent. By 1886 he had built his new brewery and the business was passed down the family until brewing ceased in 1961. The Gypsies Tent continued to trade until 1980; the building is still there.

British Oak, Salop Street, Eve Hill, Dudley:

A home brew house which was established in 1855 but had stopped brewing by 1898. Ninety years later in 1988, Ian Skitt resumed brewing and he also acquired the Spread Eagle, Lichfield Street, Bilston. Brewing ceased in 1997.

Britannia, Kent Street, Upper Gornal:

A Home brew house from 1780 until brewing stopped in 1959. It continued as a pub and in 1995 a three-barrel plant was installed. Brewing ceased again in 1997. The pub was taken over by Batham's and still trades.

Showells Crosswells Brewery, Langley:

Opened by Walter Showell in 1870 and over the next fifteen years the brewery was extended. By 1884 it had become Walter Showell & Son and six years later it acquired Taylors Hockley Brewery and Sarah Marsland Brookfield Brewery of Stockport. It acquired the Brewers Investment Corporation in 1894 giving it a total of 80 pubs. It fell prey to Samuel Allsopps Burton-on-Trent in 1914 and brewing ceased.

J.P.Simpkiss, Dennis Brewery, Brettell Lane, Brierley Hill:

Founded in 1854 by William Simpkiss as a home brew house. In 1869 his son William Henry purchased the Royal Oak, Brierley Hill and later built a brewery there. However in 1896 it was taken over by North Worcester Breweries and closed. William Henry's son Joseph Paskin purchased the Swan Brewery, Evers Street, Quarry Bank in 1903 and renamed it the Home Brewery.

However he was to lose control of it in 1916. Undaunted he purchased the Foley Arms, Brettell Lane, Brierley Hill in 1919 and started brewing. In 1934 he built a new brewery behind the pub and it traded successfully. It merged with Johnson & Phipps of

Wolverhampton in 1955 and became J.P.S. Breweries. By 1977 it had changed its name to J. P. Simpkiss & Son. In 1985 it was taken over by Greenall Whitley and the brewery closed.

Herbert Newman & Sons, 101 Pedmore, Road, Lye:

Established in 1895 next to the Seven Stars pub. It continued brewing until 1960 when it was taken over by Wolverhampton & Dudley Breweries.

North Worcester Stourbridge Brewery, Duke Street, Stourbridge:

Registered in 1886 to merge Stourbridge Rowley Brewery, Blackheath, White Swan Brewery, Oldbury and Royal Oak Brewery, Brierley Hill with 100 pubs. It carried on brewing until 1910 when after being taken over by Wolverhampton & Dudley Brewery it closed.

Premier Midland Ales, Mill Race Lane, Stoubridge:

Founded in 1988 it established seven tied houses. In 1990 it merged with Pitfield Brewery, Hoxton, London to form Pitfield Premier Brewing based at Stourbridge. The company went in to voluntary liquidation and closed in 1991.

Samuel Woodhall Brewery, High Street, West Bromwich:

Formed in 1874 it brewed at several sites in High Street over a number of years. It carried on brewing till 1937 when it was acquired by Julia Hanson, Dudley and closed.

Darbys Dunkirk Brewery, 6 Whitehall Road, Greets Green, West Bromwich:

Established 1894 it supplied beer for the local area and in 1923 became a registered company. Still wishing to expand in 1937 it acquired J.F.C. Jackson Diamond Brewery, Cromwell Street, Kates Hill, Dudley. In 1951 its brewery and 100 pubs was acquired by Mitchells & Butlers and it was closed.

Cradley Heath

Cradley Heath was the centre of the Black Country chainmaking industry. Towards the end of the last century, when trade was at its peak, around a thousand tons of chain were produced each week in Cradley Heath's workshops. As well as commercial chainshops it was common for chain to be produced as a 'cottage' industry in backyards, often by women. In 1910 the women chainmakers of Cradley Heath went on strike for better pay and conditions. This action was successful and a minimum wage was achieved.

Cradley Heath
Moon Under Water

164-166 High Street, Cradley Heath, B64 5HJ

A4100

☼ 09:00-00:00 Sun-Thu; 09:00-01:00 Fri-Sat

☎ (01384) 565419

Banks's Original; Enville Ale; Greene King Abbot Ale; Hop Back Summer Lightning; Marston's Burton Bitter, Pedigree; guest beers

Wetherspoon pub in a busy shopping area. Open-plan interior; to the rear is a pleasant paved outdoor drinking area including water feature. As usual, there are displays on local history, including some impressive chain. Food served until 11pm. Buses from Birmingham/Halesowen/Merry Hill: 138, 139; from Dudley: 243, 245. 10 minutes walk from the railway station.

Q✿❶❸ ♿ ❤❀⇌(Cradley Heath)

The Cask Marque Award

Did you know:

★ 34% of customers would go to a different outlet if quality is poor?
★ 49% would not order the same drink again if quality is poor?
★ 53% of consumers would pay more for quality?
Source: Interbrew Annual Beer Report

Cask Marque accreditation is an award that goes to licensees who serve the perfect pint of cask ale every time.

Visit **www.cask-marque.co.uk** to see a list of pubs which hold the Cask Marque Award.

CASK MARQUE

For pubs which serve the perfect pint

Darlaston

Darlaston was the nuts and bolts capital of Britain. Giant manufacturing companies with their factories here included GKN, Rubery Owen, Garringtons and F. H. Lloyd.

Darlaston

Boat
20 Bentley Road South, WS10 8LW

🕐 12:00-14:30, 18:00-23:00 Mon-Thu; 12:00-23:00 Fri; 12:00-15:00, 18:00-23:00 Sat; 12:00-15:00, 19:00-22:30 Sun

☎ (0121) 526 5104

Banks's Original, Bitter; Greene King IPA; guest beers

Two roomed 1930's canal side pub. Darts are played in the Bar. Small TV is used for sports only. Comfortable, quiet lounge. Seating available in rear garden and on front car park. Local CAMRA pub of the Year 2005.

🏚Q❀🍺♣P

Fallings Heath Tavern
248 Walsall Road, WS10 9SN

🕐 12:00-14:30, 18:00-23:00 Mon-Sat; 12:00-15:00, 19:15-22:30 Sun

☎ (0121) 526 3403

Ansells Mild, Ansells Bitter, guest beer

Three roomed roadside pub built in 1937, the comfortable lounge still has service buttons on the backs of the seats, though not in use. The bar is popular with pub games. There is a family room adjoining the garden that has bench seating. Pub still features an off licence at the front.

🐕❀🍺♣P🏠

Horse and Jockey
33 Walsall Road, WS10 9JS

🕐 11:00-23:00 Mon-Sat; 12:00-15:00, 19:30-22:30 Sun

☎ (0121) 526 4453

Banks's Original, Bitter

Two roomed pub with comfortable lounge that has prints of old paintings. The bar has photos of the pub from the first half of the last century and the family who owned it. Weekend entertainment. Benched garden play area at the rear.

Q❀🍺♣P🏠

Prince Of Wales
74 Walsall Road, WS10 9JJ

🕐 14:00-23:00 Mon-Thu; 12:00-23:00 Fri-Sat; 12:00-22:30 Sun

☎ (0121) 526 6244

Holden's Bitter, Golden Glow; guest beer

Traditional two roomed pub, darts played in long narrow bar that has a display of advertising mirrors. The lounge is small and family friendly with photos of local football teams. There is a children's play area at rear. Good value meals. Guest beer only available from Thurs each week.

❀◀🍺♣

Dudley

Dudley, the 'capital of the Black Country', was listed in the Domesday book and its castle has been a landmark for generations ever since. The Black Country was at the forefront of the Industrial Revolution and dozens of small communities sprang into being around the medieval town. Now the coal, limestone, ironstone and fireclay which supported the traditional industries have gone – along with many small, plain pubs and beer-houses which served the miners, foundry workers, chainmakers, nailmakers and glassmakers. In its time the main street through the town centre from Queens Cross to the castle gates had over 30 pubs. The social and economic history of the region can be explored at the nearby Black Country Living Museum which is also the starting point for boat trips into the Dudley tunnel and the famous limestone caverns.

Dudley: Queens Cross

Lamp Tavern

116 High Street, DY1 1QT
A461/A459 junction with Blower's Green Road

🕐 12:00-14:30, 17:00-23:00 Mon-Thu; 12:00-23:00 Fri-Sat; 12:00-22:30 Sun

☎ (01384) 254129

Batham's Mild, Best Bitter, XXX (winter)

This popular and lively pub has a large, welcoming, dog-friendly front bar, a comfortable lounge and a separate non-smoking eating area. Good value traditional pub food is served 12-2 weekday lunchtimes. Music and comedy nights are held in the former brewery building at the rear. There is a patio with views for outdoor drinking. Bed and breakfast accommodation is available in the adjacent Lamp Cottage. The pub is a 10 minute walk from Dudley bus station.

✿ ⌂ ◖ 🎇 ♣ P

Dudley: Town Centre

Full Moon

58-60 High Street, DY1 1PY

🕐 09:00-00:00 Sun-Thu; 09:00-01:00 Fri-Sat

☎ (01384) 212294

Enville Ale; Greene King Abbot Ale; Marston's Burton Bitter, Pedigree; guest beers

Wetherspoon pub in the town centre, 5 minutes walk through the market place from the bus station. Impressive in length but otherwise the usual open-plan format with historic local information. Food served until 11pm.

Q ◖ ⌂ ♣ ⊗

Old Priory

47 New Street, DY1 1LU

🕐 11:00-23:00 Mon-Sat; 12:00-22:30 Sun

☎ (01384) 455810

Banks's Original; guest beer

Originally an early 19th century home brew house called the Nags Head. Much altered over the years it is now virtually a single room but retains cosiness. Pub food is served 12:00-14:45, 18:00-21:00. It is situated conveniently for Dudley bus station.

◖ ♣

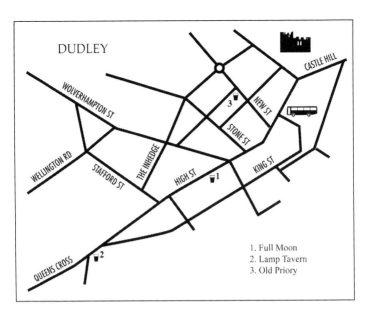

DUDLEY

WOLVERHAMPTON ST

CASTLE HILL

NEW ST

STONE ST

THE INHEDGE

WELLINGTON RD

STAFFORD ST

HIGH ST

KING ST

QUEENS CROSS

1. Full Moon
2. Lamp Tavern
3. Old Priory

Dudley Castle

Gornal

The term 'The Gornals' embraces Upper Gornal, on or near the Dudley to Sedgley road, Lower Gornal, at or near the foot of the ridge that divides the Black Country, and, further west, Gornalwood. Defining exactly where one ends and the other starts defies description. However, Gornal is the place where they put the pig on the wall to see the band go by! At one time the Gornals played their part in the local economy as the source of the much-used commodities of salt and sand.

Gornal: Lower Gornal

Black Bear
86 Deepdale Lane, DY3 2AE

Ⓒ 17:00-23:00 Mon-Thu; 16:00-23:00 Fri; 12:00-23:00 Sat; 12:00-22:30 Sun

☎ (01384) 253333
4 or more ever-changing guest beers
A former 18th century farmhouse. The split-level interior of this hillside local has eclectic charm stemming from gradual evolution. There is a small outdoor drinking area in front of the pub, providing views over Lower Gornal and beyond. Buses from Dudley/ Stourbridge: 257; from Dudley/ Wolverhampton: 541 to Robert Street then a 5 minute walk. 10 minute walk from Gornal Wood bus station.

🏨 ❁ ♣

Bulls Head
404 Himley Road, DY3 2TS
B4176/B4175 junction

Ⓒ 11:30-15:00, 18:00-23:30 Mon-Fri; 11:00-23:30 Sat; 12:00-15:00, 19:00-22:30 Sun

☎ (01384) 361102
Banks's Original, Bitter
The bar is spacious and has sport on large-screen TV. The lounge is cheerful and overlooks a small garden. There is a function room upstairs. Live music Saturday

nights. Bus from Dudley/ Stourbridge: 257. 5 minute walk from Gornal Wood bus station.

❁ ⌷ ♣ P

Five Ways
Himley Road, DY3 2PZ
B4176/B4175 junction

Ⓒ 12:00-23:30 Mon-Thu; 12:00-01:00 Fri-Sat; 12:00-23:00 Sun

☎ (01384) 252968
Batham's Best Bitter; guest beer
Single J-shaped room sweeps round from a large TV screen to a quieter lounge at the front of the pub. Small patio area at the rear. Good value food is served weekday lunchtimes. Bus from Dudley/ Stourbridge: 257. 5 minute walk from Gornal Wood bus station.

❁ ◖ ♣ P

Fountain
8 Temple Street, DY3 2PE
B4175

Ⓒ 12:00-23:00 Mon-Sat; 12:00-22:30 Sun

☎ (01384) 242777
Enville Ale; RCH Pitchfork; Greene King Abbot Ale; up to 6 guest beers
A vibrant pub with open-plan drinking areas surrounding the bar. Elevated no-smoking dining area to the rear for wholesome, reasonably priced meals, served 12-9. No food

Sun eve. Pleasant yard for outdoor drinking. The pub holds beer festivals Easter and October. Bus from Dudley/Wolverhampton: 541. 5 minute walk from Gornal Wood bus station.

●◑♣●

Old Bulls Head

1 Redhall Road, DY3 2NU
Off B4175

☉ 16:00-23:00 Mon-Fri; 12:00-23:00 Sat; 12:00-22:30 Sun

☎ (01384) 231616

www.oldbullshead.co.uk

Black Country Ales Bradley's Finest Golden, Pig on the Wall, Fireside; guest beers

Home of Black Country Ales

brewery. Impressive late Victorian building which dominates the junction with Temple Street. Internally it has a large bar and a games room. Small patio area for outside drinking. Frequent live entertainment. Cobs served. Bus from Dudley/Wolverhampton: 541. 5 minute walk from Gornal Wood bus station.

🚃●⊡♣P

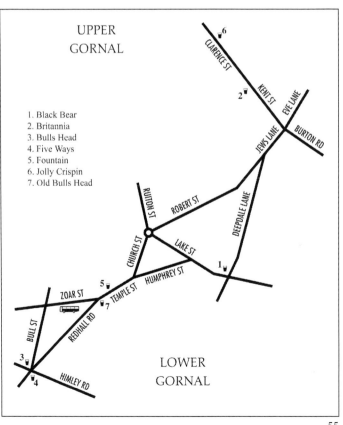

UPPER GORNAL

LOWER GORNAL

1. Black Bear
2. Britannia
3. Bulls Head
4. Five Ways
5. Fountain
6. Jolly Crispin
7. Old Bulls Head

CLARENCE ST
KENT ST
EVE LANE
BURTON RD
JEWS LANE
DEEPDALE LANE
RUITON ST
ROBERT ST
CHURCH ST
LAKE ST
HUMPHREY ST
ZOAR ST
TEMPLE ST
REDHALL RD
BULL ST
HIMLEY RD

Gornal: Upper Gornal
Britannia (Sally's)
109 Kent Street, DY3 1UX
A459

🕐 12:00-15:00, 19:00-23:00 Mon-Thu; 12:00-16:00, 19:00-23:00 Fri; 12:00-23:00 Sat; 12:00-16:00, 19:00-22:30 Sun

☎ (01902) 883253

Batham's Mild, Best Bitter, XXX (winter)

Former brew pub which was originally built in 1780 and brewed until 1959. The pub belonged to the Perry family for more than a century, until the death of Sally in 1992. At the rear is the original tap room with no bar: handpumps are set against the wall. The main servery is in the newer front bar, converted from a former butchers shop. There is also a small TV room. The backyard houses a delightful outdoor drinking area and the old brewhouse. Cobs served. Buses from Dudley/Wolverhampton: 558 stops outside; 541 to Jew's Lane then a 5 minute walk.

🏚Q🌸🍺🍀⊗

Jolly Crispin
25 Clarence Street, DY3 1UL
A459

🕐 16:00-23:00 Mon-Thu; 12:00-23:00 Fri-Sat; 12:00-15:00, 19:00-22:30 Sun

☎ (01902) 672220

www.jollycrispin.co.uk

Up to 9 ever-changing guest beers

The original part of the building dates from the 18th century. It first became a pub in 1820. The bar at the front has two cosy areas. At the rear of the building is a large comfortable lounge. CAMRA's West Midlands regional pub of the year 2005. Cobs served. Buses from Dudley/Wolverhampton: 558 stops outside; 541 to Jew's Lane then a 10 minute walk.

🍺🍽P

REAL ALE

Ah luv a drink of traditional brew
Pint after pint yoe shud see it goo;
Brewed from barley, malt, hops and yeast
It's better than any expensive feast.
Fust ther's maltin, millin an mashin
Boilin and coolin it sure teks a bashin;
Ther's still moower ter goo: it's called fermentation
Nah it ony needs rackin ter sell ter the Nation.

From brewery ter pub in a cask of wood or metal
It must stop in the cellar an gid time ter settle;
Ter let aht the gas cuzz the beers still alive
Is plaircied at the top a vent hole or shive
In which a porous wood peg known as a spile
Is knocked into position to remain in for a while.
A tap is then ommered into a bung
The cask is now ready or con summat goo wrung?

Well, it's rarely drunk by gravity these days
So it cums through the pipes in a number of ways
Involving an 'ond pump with manual strairn
Or electrically powered does exactly the sairme.
Mind yoe, ther's brewers who use C.O.2
With blanket an top pressure pushin it through;
The pipes from the cellar must be clane an kept right
And stored at 54 to 57 degrees Fahrenheit.

Various types an tairsts of beers am med
In flagons, kilderkins, barrels an hogs yeds
Ther's bitters, milds, stouts and strunger stuff
Yoe con drink til yoe drap or just 'ave enuff;
Alcohol by volume 4, 5, 6, percentage or moower
Drink too much an yoe'll be hitting the flewer
But mek sure it ay cloudy cuzz this ay a loff
Yoe'll end up wi' bally airche an 'ave ter trot off.

Keg on the other 'ond ay wuth a mention
It's filtered an pasteurised with a fizzy retention
An lagers the sairme it's just as jed
All that seems ter gi' yer is a pain in the yed;
So when ya wazzin's dry as a boon
Nip dahn ya local ter any bar room
An whether it's dark or whether it's pale
Wotever yoe'm avin mek it REAL ALE.

By Peter Hill

Halesowen

The original Anglo-Saxon settlement of Halas on the River Stour became Halas-Owen in the 12th Century after it was given to one of the medieval Lords of the Manor. The Abbots of St. Mary's eventually acquired control and granted a market and Borough status. The ruins of the Abbey, just South of the town centre, are sometimes open to the public in Summertime, but the parish church of St. John – partly dating to Norman times – is more likely to catch the visitor's eye. Sir William Shenstone, the 'father of English landscape gardening', is buried in the churchyard. He laid out Leasowes Park in the 18th Century. The park has enjoyed lottery-funded restoration and is within walking distance of the town centre.

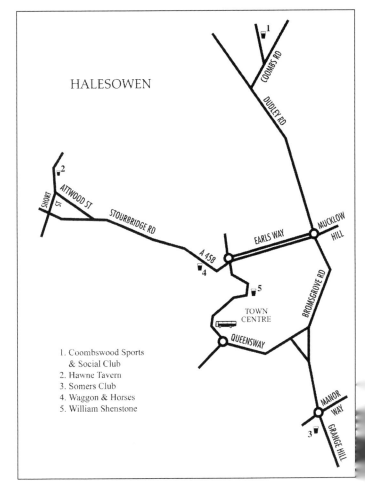

1. Coombswood Sports
   & Social Club
2. Hawne Tavern
3. Somers Club
4. Waggon & Horses
5. William Shenstone

Halesowen

Coombs Wood Sports and Social Club

Lodgfield Road, Halesowen, B62 8AA

Just off A4099 Halesowen to Blackheath rd

☼ 19:30-23:00 Mon-Thu; 19:00-23:00 Fri; 12:30-23:00 Sat; 12:00-22:30 Sun

☎ (0121) 561 1932

Beer range varies

Formerly the social club for the local steel works, the steel works has long gone. Fortunately, the social club continues to thrive, being the base for various sports teams and lying adjacent to a bowling green and cricket pitch. The single room has a pool table at one end and a big screen at the other. Visitors should carry a copy of this guide or a current CAMRA membership card.

Hawne Tavern

76 Attwood Street, B63 3UG

200 yards from A458, near Halesowen Town FC

☼ 16:30-23:00 Mon-Fri; 12:00-23:00 Sat; 12:00-10:30 Sun

☎ (0121) 602 2601

Banks's Bitter, Batham's Best Bitter, guest beers

Friendly side-street Victorian tavern 3/4 mile from the town centre, close to the frequent no 9 bus route and Halesowen Town FC. Two regular and up to six guests are served in a cosy lounge (ideal for a quiet pint) and a stable-type bar with a separate pool table area and a small patio area that also hosts the occasional beer festival. Former Stourbridge CAMRA Pub of the Year and has featured regularly in the national CAMRA Good Beer Guide.

Q❀⏦♣P✠

Somers Sports & Social Club

The Grange, Grange Hill, B62 0JH
(at A456/B4551 jct)

🕐 12:00-14:30, 18:00-23:00 Mon-Sat; 12:00-14:00, 19:00-22.30 Sun

☎ (0121) 550 1645

Banks's Bitter; Batham's Mild, Best Bitter; Olde Swan Original; Taylor Landlord; guest beers

This three-times winner of CAMRA's national club of the year lies on the green belt side of the by-pass and occupies a large 250 year old house. Seating is comfy in all areas, with a large patio overlooking the bowling green. Please show this guide or a CAMRA membership card to gain admission. Groups of five or more must call ahead. Bus routes 9, 241 pass the club.

Q🛏️❀P

Waggon & Horses

21 Stourbridge Road, B63 3TU
On A458, five minutes walk from bus stn.

🕐 12:00-23:00 Mon-Sat, 12:00-22:30 Sun

☎ (0121) 550 4989

Batham's Best Bitter; Oakham White Dwarf; Windsor Castle Worcester Sorcerer; Nottingham EPA; Bank Top Dark Mild; guest beers

Any visitor to the Black Country must add the Waggon onto their itinerary - the pub is a legend in the local area and further afield, probably due to the vast beer range and the welcoming bar staff. In addition to the five regulars, up to ten guests have long provided an unrivalled choice in the area. At each end of the long row of hand pumps on the bar is a quieter area allowing escape from the bustle

of the main bar. A quiz is held alternative Wednesday evenings in aid of the West Midlands Air Ambulance. Good quality home made sandwiches are freshly made to order 12pm - 5pm and unusual crisps and snacks are available at any time. To complement the ales, fruit wines and draught Belgian beers are sold.

Q

William Shenstone

1-5 Queensway, B63 4AB
Right next door to bus stn, opp. Church.

🕐 09:00-00:00 Sun-Thu; 09:00-01:00 Fri-Sat

☎ (0121) 585 6246

www.jdwetherspoon.co.uk

Beer range varies

Lively Wetherspoons free house in the town centre with a good range of ales including some local choices. As usual, smokers, non-smokers and families are catered for. The familiar good value JDW menu is also available.

◐◖♿⊗

Kingswinford

The original village was next to St Mary's Church on the Dudley road. The centre of activity now is ¼ mile away at the Cross where the Dudley road meets the Stourbridge –Wolverhampton road. Here are shops, restaurants and other facilities. Broadfield House Glass Museum in Compton Drive contains glass from the Roman period right up to the present day, but the emphasis is on the history of glass production in the local areas of Amblecote, Wordsley, Brierley Hill and Stourbridge. There is an integral studio where glassmaking is demonstrated.

Kingswinford
Bridge

110 Moss Grove, DY6 9HH
A491

☺ 12:00-15:00, 17:00-23:30 Mon-Thu;
12:00-23:45 Fri-Sat; 12:00-23:30 Sun

☎ (01384) 352356

Banks's Original, Bitter; guest beers
This welcoming pub is housed in a Grade II listed building. A comfortable bar extends across the front. Behind is a cosy lounge with real fire. Outside is a well-equiped garden which is augmented by barbeques and bouncy castle in summer. Occasional live entertainment at weekends. Sandwiches made to order. Buses from Dudley: 261; from Stourbridge/Wolverhampton: 256. 10 minutes walk from the centre of Kingswinford.

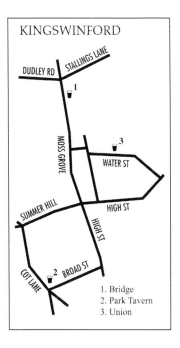

KINGSWINFORD

1. Bridge
2. Park Tavern
3. Union

Park Tavern

182 Cot Lane, DY6 9QG

Off A4101 & A491

☏ 12:00-23:00 Mon-Sat; 12:00-15:00, 19:00-23:00 Sun

☎ (01384) 287178

Tetley Bitter; Batham's Best Bitter; guest beer

Two-roomed locals pub. The bar clientele are sports-oriented: sky TV and darts feature here. The lounge is popular with people who want a quiet drink and chat. There is a small terrace for outdoor drinking. The Broadfield House glass museum is nearby. Buses from Dudley: 264/265, 274/275; from Stourbridge: 267. 10 minute walk from Kingswinford centre.

❀◱♣P

Union

54 Water Street, DY6 7QB

Off A4101/A491

☏ 12:00-15:00, 18:00-23:00 Mon-Thu; 12:00-23:00 Fri-Sat; 12:00-22:30 Sun

☎ (01384) 293061

Banks's Original, Bitter; guest beer

A small late-Victorian pub set in a back street. The main, L-shaped room is comfortable and friendly and popular for crib, dominoes and darts. There is a non-smoking snug where children are welcome up to 9pm. The pub also boasts a pleasant walled garden. Cobs served (not Sun). It is 10 minutes walk from the centre of Kingswinford which is served by several bus routes from Dudley, Stourbridge and Wolverhampton.

☙❀♣❀P⊟

Brewers Of Genuine Beers Since 1877

www.bathams.co.uk

THE BLACK COUNTRY
GOOD BEER GUIDE AREA

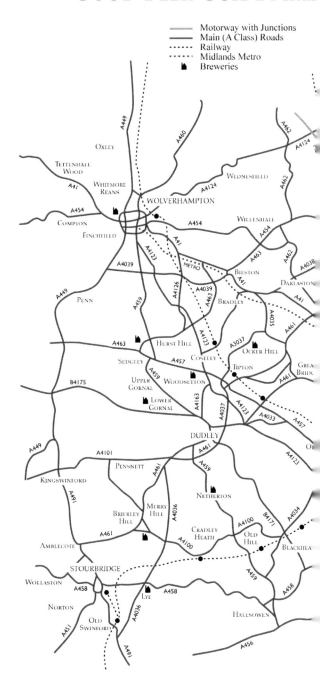

	Legend
	Motorway with Junctions
	Main (A Class) Roads
	Railway
	Midlands Metro
	Breweries

KINVER BREWERY

Regular Beers

Plus seasonal ales, including the award winning:

Contact
Ian - 07906 146777
Dave - 07715 842679
Email: kinvercave@aol.com
www.kinverbrewery.co.uk

BIGGER IS
NOT ALWAYS
BETTER...

UNLESS YOU WIN SOME OF THE BIGGEST AWARDS IN THE INDUSTRY.

Voted '2005 Midland Mild of the year' CAMRA, '2004 Mild of the year' SIBA and three times winner at the International Brewing Awards. Judges from around the world agree that Highgate Dark Mild is big on taste.

We've been producing ales from the nations heart for over 100 years. Small enough to keep in touch with our drinkers, but big enough to serve leading pub companies across the UK.

This is one instance where bigger is better.

THE MIDLANDS NUMBER ONE 'DARK MILD'
WWW.HIGHGATEBREWERY.COM • 01922 644453
National deliveries available

Netherton

Netherton was an intensive mining area, with the associated ironworks and furnaces. Noah Hingley & Sons' products included anchors, most notably that for the Titanic. At the other extreme, the company of John Barnsley was famous for manufacturing Jews Harps. Joe Darby, born in Netherton in 1861, was a spring jumper who performed amazing feats from a standing start. A modern statue of him is sited in the centre of Netherton and is regularly clothed by the locals.

Bumble Hole

Netherton

Olde Swan (Ma Pardoe's)

89 Halesowen Road, DY2 9PY
In Netherton centre on A459 Dudley-Old Hill road

🕐 11:00-23:00 Mon-Sat; 12:00-16:00, 19:00-22:30 Sun

☎ (01384) 253075

Olde Swan Original, Dark Swan, Entire, Bumblehole, seasonal beers
Characterful pub on CAMRA's National Inventory of historic pub interiors. Home of Olde Swan Brewery. Runner up in CAMRA national pub of the year competition 2004. The front bar is an unspoilt gem, with enamelled ceiling, and there is a cosy rear snug. The restaurant, originally the shop next door, caters for all tastes with its varied menu, including Black Country favourites. Diners are advised to book. Lower age limit of 14. No meals Sun eve. There is a pleasant yard for outdoor drinking. The pub was kept by Frederick Pardoe from 1932 until 1952 when his widow Doris took over, until her death in 1984. Buses from Dudley: 243, 244, 245, 247, 283; from Halesowen: 244,248; from Cradley Heath railway station: 243, 245.

🏨Q🌸🌗🍴🛏P🚫

Oldbury

Historically, Oldbury has been very closely connected with Halesowen and belonged to Halesowen Abbey from the 13th century to the dissolution. It owes its industrial prominence to its mineral resources, now exhausted, and to its position on James Brindley's Birmingham Canal, completed in 1772. The coming of the canal enabled Birmingham firms to move to new sites in the Black Country where there was greater room for expansion. Manufacturing output remains diverse, but particular mention should be made to the chemical works at Langley, established at the beginning of the 20th century. Also at Langley is the site of the late-19th century maltings of Banks's brewery. Oldbury town centre houses the modern council house of Sandwell Metropolitan Borough.

Oldbury: Langley
Crosswells
Whyley Walk, B69 4SB
Off Station Road (B4182)
☉ 12:00-23:30 Mon-Fri; 12:00-00:00 Sat; 12:00-22:30 Sun

☎ (0121) 552 2626
Banks's Original; Marston's Pedigree; Olde Swan Entire; guest beer
The pub has two bar areas, a lounge with no-smoking area, a carvery restaurant and a live music/big screen TV function room, making it popular with a variety of clientele. The restaurant is open 11am to 9pm Mon-Sat and 12am to 7pm Sun. The pub is 5 minutes walk from the Titford Canal. Bus from Dudley/Birmingham:120. Langley Green railway station is 10 minutes walk away.
◑ ⏣ ♿ P ⊗ ≢ (Langley Green)

Model
2 Titford Road, B69 4PZ
Off Station Road (B4182)
☉ 11:30-23:00 Mon-Thu; 11:30-00:00 Fri-Sat; 11:00-23:00 Sun

☎ (0121) 532 0090
Greene King Abbot Ale; Taylor Landlord; guest beer
Originally the Queens Head, this pub was known as the Model because of its Frederick Smith's Model Brewery etched windows, one of which remains. Pool and large screen TV dominate one side of the U-shaped single room whilst the other side caters for diners, including a non-smoking conservatory. Pub menu plus evening specials. Food served 12-2, 5:30-9 Mon-Sat; 12-3 Sun. Children and dogs welcome. There is a beer garden in the yard. The pub is 5 minutes walk from the Titford Canal. Bus from Dudley/Birmingham:120. Langley Green railway station is 10 minutes walk away.
🏨 ⊛ ◑ ♣ P ⊗ ≢ (Langley Green)

Oldbury: Town Centre
Waggon & Horses

17A Church Street, B69 3AD
Off A4034

☉ 12:00-23:00 Mon-Thu;12:00-00:00

Fri-Sat; 12:00-22:30 Sun

☎ (0121) 552 5467

Enville White; Oakham JHB; guest beers

This pub's splendid tiled walls, panelled ceiling and Holt Brewery etched windows contribute to its place on CAMRA's National Inventory of historic pub interiors. Several drinking areas are frequented by office workers and locals alike. Pub meals served Mon-Sat lunchtimes 12-2:30. Buses from Birmingham, Dudley and West Bromwich stop close by. 10 minutes walk from Sandwell & Dudley railway station.

🏬🕺◀P✪⇌(Sandwell & Dudley)

Oldbury: Warley
Plough

George Road, B68 9LN
Off A4123

☉ 14:00-23:00 Mon-Thu; 14:00-00:00

Fri; 12:00-00:00 Sat; 12:00-23:00 Sun

☎ (0121) 552 3822

Adnams Bitter; Banks's Original; Marston's Pedigree; guest beer

This community-focused local began life as a farmhouse and retains a rustic feel. The lounge has four cosy drinking areas on different levels. The bar is sports-orientated. There is a pleasant garden behind the pub. Bus from Birmingham/Oldbury/Blackheath: 128 stops outside; more frequent bus service from Birmingham/Dudley: 126 to Wolverhampton Road then a 10 minute walk up Brandhall Road.

🌸🍺♣P

Langley Maltings

Pelsall

Pelsall retains the feel of a village, with a remarkable finger post on the main road. It was originally an Anglo-Saxon settlement.

Pelsall
Old Bush
Walsall Road, WS3 4BP

🕐 12:00-23:00 Mon-Sun

☎ (01922) 423690

Wells Bombardier; guest beers

This lively pub benefits from pleasant views over Pelsall Common. The base for many activities including football teams and folk music, the interior consists of a rustic themed bar and a split level lounge / restaurant. A small patio area at the side of the pub can be used by drinkers in summer.

🕷◗ P

Railway Inn
Victoria Road, WS3 4BH

🕐 12:00-15:00, 18:00-23:00 Mon-Fri; 12:00-23:00 Sat; 12:00-10:30 Sun

☎ (01922) 686911

Beer range varies

Comfortable village pub with far reaching views over Pelsall common. Popular with drinkers and diners alike, with good quality food served in the traditional style lounge. The separate bar is host to darts teams and the pub holds a weekly Monday night quiz.

◗♣P

Teach Yourself How To Speak Black Country

For many people, the sound of the West Midlands is still Amy Turtle on Crossroads, Barry in Auf Wiedersehen Pet and Jasper Carrott (who is actually from Birmingham). The Black Country dialect is said to be very close to old English and, just as in mining areas where dialects can be linked to specific pits, the West Midlands dialects differ from one small town to another. Bilston near Wolverhampton is different to Dudley and Walsall, and woe betide you if you ask someone in their Black Country local if they are a Brummie.

Correct pronunciation is important. In the Black Country "boil" would be pronounced "bile" as in "bile the kettle", "bake" would be pronounced "baerk", as in "baerk a caerk". Two characters who feature in many local tales and jokes are Aynuk and Ayli. The following story will give you a starting point:

Aynuk: What's the difference between a buffalo and a bison?

Ayli: I dunno, I've never washed me 'onds in a buffalo.

Teaching languages in the Black Country must be a nightmare: the kids will be confused when they see a verb conjugated as "I am, you are, he is, we are, they are" because here it's "I am, yow bist, he bin".

Consider the following ...

A Chinese person might give their name as "Yow Min Lye", only to be told "No mate: yow min Brierley Hill."

This sad tale gives further insight into Black Country verbs:

Aynuk: Oh Ayli. We'm in trouble. I just saw a chap mekkin' off wi' me car.

Ayli: Strike! ..t'ay 'alf a problem.

Aynuk: Do' fret though ... I got the number as it drove off.

Ayli's response introduced the negative, which conjugates as "I ay, Yo ay, He ay" and so on. No, the 'h' isn't always missed: it's optional.

To conclude, let me provide you with a few useful phrases to try out on the locals:

Ordering refreshment: a point of moild (or, a pointer Bonks's)
Approval of pint: this is bosting (or, this ay 'alf good)
Greetings: y'oright? (or, 'ow bin yer?)
Farewells: terrar a bit

These few phrases should serve you well and allow you to slip unnoticed in and out of the Black Country and its praiseworthy hostelries. However, should any of your efforts meet with the response "you'm saft", this is probably a good time to move on or buy several people a drink. Following and understanding other people's conversations can be difficult, especially in areas like Bilston where the dialect is broad. However if you hear something like "e's a bit of a saft bogger" or "that wench is as green as 'ers cabbage looking", your cover may have been blown.

Mine's a moild!

Jokes from "Aynuk and Ayli's Black Country Joke Book" by Douglas Parker, published by Broadside, Tettenhall, Wolverhampton. Used with author's permission.

Pensnett

Pensnett Chase once stretched from Kingswinford in the west to Netherton in the east. The area became industrialized with mining, brickmaking and iron working. An early railway was constructed to service the industry. The first steam locomotive to run in the Black Country, the Agenoria, worked on the Shutt End railway in Pensnett from 1829. Today a large modern trading estate houses a pit head frame from the area's past. Barrow Hill, located in Pensnett, is a conspicuous landscape feature made of a dome-shaped mass of dolerite which is a hard dark grey/black igneous rock formed underneath what was once the Dudley volcano.

Pensnett

Fox & Grapes

176 High Street, DY5 4JQ
A4101

🕐 11:00-23:00 Mon-Thu; 12:00-23:00

Fri-Sat; 12:00-22:30 Sun

☎ (01384) 261907

Batham's Mild, Best Bitter, XXX (winter)

Acquired by Bathams to replace the nearby Holly Bush which was closed in 1999 and demolished for housing. Inside the striking brick frontage a Bathams tiled passageway leads to several drinking areas around a central bar. There is a lawn with benches to the rear and a patio at the front overlooking the main road. Buses from Dudley: 261, 264/265, 274/275; from Halesowen/Old Hill/Cradley Heath/Merry Hill shopping centre:138 (evenings only) to High Oak and a 10 minute walk.

🍺🌸♣P

Rushall

Rushall was an established Manor mentioned in the Domesday Book. Rushall Hall dates largely from the 19th Century, but the original fortified gateway and walls survive. In the Civil War the hall was under siege, and eventually taken by the King's Royalists before being taken back later.

Rushall

Manor Arms

Park Road, off Daw End Lane, WS4 1LQ

Off B4154 At Canal Bridge

☼ 12:00-23:00 Mon-Sat; 12:00-22:30 Sun

☎ (01922) 642333

Banks's Original, Bitter; guest beer

Grade II Listed building in attractive canalside setting. Three small quaint rooms including a bar room without a counter. Lovely grassy outdoor drinking area. A country pub right in town. Adjacent to Park Lime Pits nature reserve.

♒Q❀❀⊟♣P

Sedgley

Sedgley was the centre of a large manor which included what is now Coseley and stretched as far as, and included, Dudley Castle. Today it is a pleasant residential area with shops in the streets around the Bull Ring. Beacon Hill is the end of the dividing ridge of the Black Country and is the site of a stone signal tower, originally built during the 19th century as an astronomical observatory.

Sedgley
Beacon Hotel
129 Bilston Street, DY3 1JE
A463

☼ 12:00-14:30, 17:30-23:00 Mon-Fri; 12:00-15:00, 18:00-23:00 Sat; 12:00-15:00, 19:00-22:30 Sun

☎ (01902) 883380
Sarah Hughes Pale Amber, Sedgley Surprise, Dark Ruby, Snowflake (winter); 2 ever-changing guest beers
Restored Victorian brewery and pub full of character. The original 3 tier tower brewery at the rear was re-opened in 1987 after 30 years closure. The award-winning 'Ruby Mild' is brewed to a family recipe over 100 years old. The pub is included in CAMRA's National Inventory of historic pub interiors Four distinctive rooms are served via hatchways from a tiny central bar. There's a conservatory, unusually full of plants. Yard, garden and children's play area outside. Cobs served. Buses from Dudley/Wolverhampton: 545 stops outside; 541, 558 to Sedgley centre then a 10 minute walk.
Q�⚫♣P

Bulls Head
27 Bilston Street, DY3 1JA
A463

☼ 10:00-23:30 Mon-Sat; 11:00-23:30 Sun

☎ (01902) 578905
Holden's Bitter, Golden Glow, Special, seasonal beers
This community pub has a open-plan, L-shaped layout. The boisterous bar area to the front contrasts with the more sedate, raised, lounge area to the rear. Rolls served. Buses from Dudley/Wolverhampton: 545 stops outside; 541, 558 to Sedgley centre then a 5 minute walk.
♣

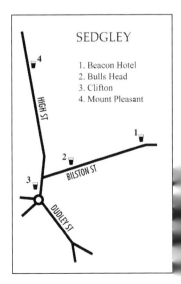

SEDGLEY

1. Beacon Hotel
2. Bulls Head
3. Clifton
4. Mount Pleasant

Clifton

Bull Ring, DY3 1LX

A459

🕙 09:00-00:00 Sun-Thu; 09:00-01:00 Fri-Sat

☎ (01902) 677448

Enville Ale; Greene King Abbot Ale; Highgate Davenports Bitter, Dark Mild; Marston's Pedigree; guest beers

This pub stands on the Bull Ring roundabout in the village centre. It is a Wetherspoon conversion of a former cinema and the Odeon-style frontage has been retained. Internally there are varied levels of drinking areas and there is also a outdoor area adjoining the side road. Food is served until 11pm. Buses from Dudley/Wolverhampton: 541, 545, 558.

Q🌑◐🕭🍎P🚷

Mount Pleasant (Stump)

144 High Street, DY3 1RH

A459

🕙 18:00-23:00 Mon-Sat; 12:00-15:00, 18:00-22:30 Sun

☎ (07999) 340524

Up to 6 guest beers, usually including one or more from RCH

Freehouse with a bar to the front and cosy lounge areas to the rear. No smoking throughout except for back corridor. Cobs served. Bus from Dudley/Wolverhampton: 558. Half mile from Sedgley centre heading towards Wolverhampton.

🏟🍺♣🚷

Smethwick

Once described as 'an insignificant hamlet', Smethwick had become an important manufacturing centre producing a wide variety of goods by the late 19th century. Industrialists were quick to take advantage of the large areas of land alongside the Birmingham to Wolverhampton Main Line canal to build foundries and workshops. Much of the glass and ironwork used in the construction of the Crystal Palace was produced in Smethwick's factories. The area around the canals, known as the Galton Valley, has been developed recently as a part of the region's industrial heritage. Its centrepiece is the cast-iron Galton Bridge, constructed in the 1820s to span the deep cutting of Thomas Telford's new line canal.

Smethwick: Bearwood

Dog

8 Hagley Road West, B67 5EU
A456

○ 11:00-23:00 Mon-Thu; 11:00-01:00 Fri-Sat; 11:30-23:00 Sun

☎ (0121) 434 6921

M&B Brew XI; Marston's Pedigree; Taylor Landlord; guest beer

Surrounded by Lightwoods Park, this old building has been modernised internally. It is open-plan but with varied seating areas. The menu offers good choice and food is served until 8pm. Children over the age of 14 are admitted if dining; any age is welcome in the patio garden. Buses from Dudley/Birmingham: 126, 140; from Halesowen/Birmingham: 9, 19, 109, 138, 139; other services to Bearwood bus station and a 5 minute walk.

🌑🌓 P ⊗

Smethwick: Uplands

Old Chapel

2 The Uplands, B67 6EQ
Between A4030 and B4182

○ 11:00-23:00 Mon-Wed; 11:00-23:30 Thu, Sun; 11:00-00:30 Fri-Sat

☎ (0121) 555 4900

M&B Mild, Brew XI

The oldest non-religious building in Smethwick, probably built soon after the neighbouring church which was consecrated in 1732. First documented in 1818 when it was named the Hand of Providence. The building has been Grade II listed since 1947. Large bar popular for pub games; cosy lounge; pleasant garden with bowling green. Basic good value food is served 12-2 Mon-Sun; 6-8 Mon-Fri. Bus from Birmingham/Blackheath: 88.

🌑🌓🚪♣

Galton Bridge

Black Country Canals

The Industrial Revolution of the late 18th Century led to a great demand locally for the raw materials of coal, fireclay, and iron ore. The problem was transporting them to the factories and foundries that needed them. This was solved by the introduction of canals, which enabled large quantities to be carried more quickly than they could have been by the poor quality roads in existence at the time. These canals also facilitated the transportation of the finished goods.

The first canal in the Black Country to open was the stretch between Birmingham and Wednesbury, opened in 1769. Its purpose was to serve the already existing ironworks and mines in the district. Designed by James Brindley, this followed a meandering route, and was the first stage of the Birmingham Canal Company's plans to connect Birmingham with Wolverhampton and the Staffordshire and Worcestershire Canal (also under construction at the same time). Both were completed in 1772. The Birmingham Canal 'Main Line' was so successful that several arms and a branch canal to Walsall through Great Bridge were constructed. The amount of traffic on the Birmingham Canal became a problem, as was the water supply, especially at Smethwick, where the summit level was later lowered to cut out six locks. This work was designed by John Smeaton.

In 1776 Acts were passed for two new canals, one from Stourbridge to join the Staffs and Worcs at Stourton, west of Stourbridge, and the Dudley Canal to link it with Dudley, and beyond there the original 'Main Line'. This involved the construction of the Delph

Locks in Brierley Hill near the Batham's brewery tap The Vine, and the Dudley Tunnel. This was finally completed in 1785, joining the Main Line at Tipton. An Act of 1793 permitted a canal to join the southern end of Dudley Tunnel to Selly Oak in Birmingham via the notorious Lapal Tunnel to the east of Halesowen. Wyrley and Essington (known as the 'Curly Wyrley') was given the go ahead in 1792, linking Wolverhampton and Wyrley in Staffordshire, via Wednesfield and Bloxwich. In 1794 permission was granted to extend the main canal eastwards into Brownhills. The Walsall Branch Canal was completed in 1840 connecting the Wyrley and Essington to the Birmingham company's canal system.

Between 1825 and 1838, under Thomas Telford's instructions, a new Birmingham 'Main Line' was constructed between Deepfields, Coseley and Birmingham. This was to alleviate the previous difficulties with congestion and water supply. This new line involved huge cuttings and embankments, but cut 7 miles off the journey from Birmingham to Wolverhampton. Evidence of the three different levels of the main lines can be seen in Smethwick, although only two of them are still navigable.

Boat emerging from Netherton Tunnel

By 1846 both the Wyrley and Essington and Dudley Canal companies had amalgamated with the Birmingham Canal Navigations (BCN), forming a network of over 100 miles of waterways. It was about this time that the railway companies had taken control of the canals. Although trade with other regions fell, that of the locality did not, and expansion was needed. The 3,027 yard long Netherton Tunnel was built in 1858 to relieve the pressure of traffic through Dudley. Parallel to the Dudley Tunnel, which had no towpath and was restricted to one-way traffic, the new tunnel had towpaths both sides and was wide enough for two-way traffic.

At the end of the 19th Century, around 9 million tons of goods per year were being carried on the BCN, but with faster rail and road transport this gradually diminished: by the 1950's it had shrunk to 1 million tons. Ten years later the waterways were hardly used at all and many fell into irreversible disrepair. All is not gloom and doom, however.

Delph Locks

Today, much of the Black Country's canal network still remains navigable, thanks to the contributions of volunteers and enthusiasts, who from the late 1960's began the task of reclaiming our watery heritage. The Inland Waterways Association, along with many local organizations including the Dudley Canal Trust, the Coombeswood Canal Trust, the Lapal Canal Trust, and the BCN Society, must be congratulated and supported for their contributions.

At its zenith the BCN had about 180 miles of waterways of which roughly two-thirds still exist in varying degrees of navigability. As well as industry growing along the banks of these canals, pubs sprang up and many still remain, which is just what you need when walking the towpaths or boating at a leisurely pace.

Boat at Bumble Hole

Stourbridge

Stourbridge developed in the Middle Ages around this important river crossing and expanded in the 17th Century when Stourbridge 'ironmongers' became important in the iron trade and secured lucrative contracts to supply the navy with weapons and ironware. One of these was Robert Foley who lived in what is now the Talbot Hotel in the High Street. The first commercial locomotive to run on rails in the U.S.A. – the Stourbridge Lion – was manufactured in the town in the 1820's. A 1930's replica and the original boiler are on display in American museums. Notable buildings include the restored Bonded Warehouse and the Victorian Town Hall, where the Stourbridge Beer Festival is held.

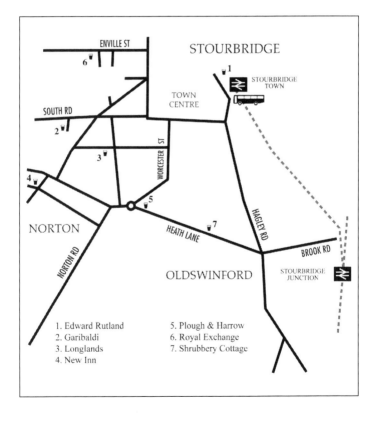

1. Edward Rutland
2. Garibaldi
3. Longlands
4. New Inn
5. Plough & Harrow
6. Royal Exchange
7. Shrubbery Cottage

Stourbridge

Edward Rutland

77 - 78 High Street, DY8 1DX
In the High St next to bus / rail interchange

🕐 11:00-01:00 Mon-Sat; 12:00-00:30 Sun

☎ (01384) 445670
www.jdwetherspoon.co.uk
Beer range varies
Part of the Lloyds No 1 sub chain of JD Wetherspoon pubs. Serving food and playing loud music during the evening. Late night drinkers can get a decent pint here.

◑ 🚻 ⧧

Garibaldi

19 Cross Street, DY8 3XE
Just outside town centre in the 'Old Quarter'.

🕐 12:00-23:00 Mon-Sat; 12:00-16:30, 19:00-22:30 Sun

☎ (01384) 373390 www.thegaribaldi.info

Banks's Original, Bitter; Marston's Pedigree
This pub is hard to find but worth the effort. Three rooms provide a choice for alternative tastes. The traditional bar offers cards and darts, while the more energetic can play pool in the family room. Real live music featuring local and overseas performers can often be found in the comfortable lounge. Details on web site.

🛏 ⛁ ♣ P

Longlands Tavern

24 Western Road, DY8 3XU
Walking distance, SW of town centre.

🕐 13:00-23:00 Mon-Thu; 12:00-23:00 Fri-Sat; 12:00-22:30 Sun

☎ (01384) 392073

Banks's Original, Bitter
Small Banks's pub tucked away in the residential 'Old Quarter', this pub was the birthplace of the Stourbridge branch of CAMRA with its first meeting taking place here. The layout is comfy lounge and traditional bar where pub games are enjoyed by a mixed clientele. It is home to many games teams including Petanque and a quiz team. A function room upstairs is available to hire with a buffet if required.

✿ ⛁ 🚻 ♣

Royal Exchange

75 Enville Street, DY8 1XW
Just outside Ring Road on A458 towards Wollaston

🕐 13:00-23:00 Mon-Fri (12:00-23:00 in Summer); 12:00-23:00 Sat, 12:00-22:30 Sun

☎ (01384) 396726

Batham's Mild, Bitter, seasonal beers
This terraced pub is a half mile walk from the Bus/Rail stn and is opposite a free car park. It has a lively bar decorated with Irish themed pictures, a small cosy lounge and a large patio for warm summer evenings. An upstairs function room is used by various groups and is available for hire. Daytime home-made cobs available. Stowford Press Westons Cider is on draught and Westons Organic is also available. Former Stourbridge CAMRA Pub of the Year.

Q ✿ ⛁ ♣ ◑ P ⧧

Stourbridge: Amblecote

Maverick

Brettell Lane, DY8 4BA
On junction of A491 and A461

🕐 12:00-00:00 Mon,Tue,Thu; 12:00-01:00 Wed,Fri,Sat; 12:00-23:00 Sun

☎ (01384) 824099

Banks's Bitter, Two ever-changing guest ales

This pub welcomes all age groups, including families. It has a wild west décor, a Mexican room and a beer garden. Live music is a regular feature. Styles include folk, blues, roots and bluegrass. Sports fans can watch their favourite game on Sky TV. A pool table and darts board are available for the more energetic.

Robin Hood

196 Collis Street, DY8 3EQ
On A4102 (one-way) off A461 Brettell Ln.

🕐 12:00-15:00, 18:00-23:00 Mon-Fri; 12:00-23:00 Sat; 12:00-22:30 Sun

☎ (01384) 821120

Batham's Best Bitter; Enville Ale; Salopian Shropshire Gold; four guest beers

On the main Brierley Hill to Stourbridge road, close to buses, noted for its excellent home-cooked lunchtime and evening menu. A quiz is held on the first Tuesday every month. En-suite accommodation available.

🌸 ➡◖◗ P

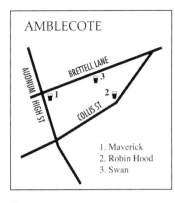

AMBLECOTE

1. Maverick
2. Robin Hood
3. Swan

Swan

10 Brettel Lane, DY8 4BN
On A461 towards Dudley on RHS, 1/3 mile after A491

🕐 12:00-14:30, 19:00-23:00 Mon,Fri; 19:00-23:00 Tue-Thu; 12:00-23:00 Sat; 12:00-15:00, 19:00-22:30 Sun

☎ (01384) 76932

Three ever-changing guest beers

This friendly two roomed pub has a comfortable lounge and a basic public bar where traditional pub games are played. Regular raffles are held for local charities and the Air Ambulance. The garden is a delightful sun trap and provides an ideal setting for sampling the well kept ales on offer.

🌸◖◗♣

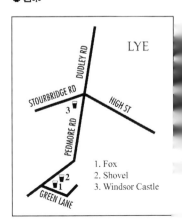

LYE

1. Fox
2. Shovel
3. Windsor Castle

Stourbridge: Lye

Fox

8 Green Lane, DY9 7EW

Just off A4036, 1/3 mile south of Lye
Cross / stn.

☉ 15:00-23:00 Mon-Fri; 11:00-23:00
Sat; 12:00-22:30 Sun

☎ (01384) 898614

Banks's Original, Bitter

Situated in a narrow side-street,
the pub has served the local
community for many years. In
the large bar area, darts, crib and
dominoes are played daily. There is
also a comfortable lounge.

Shovel

81 Pedmore Road, DY9 7DZ

On A4036, just south of the Cross

☉ 17:00-00:00 Mon-Thu; 15:00-00:00
Fri; 14:00-00:00 Sat; 12:00-00:00 Sun

☎ (01384) 423998

www.theshovelinn.co.uk

Batham's Best Bitter; guest beers

Two-roomed free house serving
popular food. Several alcoves and
side areas allow space for a quiet
drink if that's what you desire.

Windsor Castle

7 Stourbridge Road, Lye, DY9 7DG

Right on the cross

☉ 12:00-23:00 Mon-Sun

☎ (01384) 897809

www.windsorcastlebrewery.com

Full Windsor Castle range

Windsor Castle Brewery tap which
opened in spring 2006. Food is
served all day until 9pm, after
which you can bring in a takeaway
curry from across the road.

Stourbridge: Norton

New Inn

2 Cherry Street, Norton, DY8 3YQ

Off B4186 via Glebe Lane.

☉ 15:00-23:00 Mon-Thu; 14:00-23:00
Fri; 12:00-23:00 Sat; 12:00-23:00 Sun

☎ (01384) 393323

www.newinnstourbridge.com

**Adnams Bitter; Draught Bass;
Enville Ale; Greene King IPA, Abbot
Ale**

Popular local, traditional two
room pub, smart throughout. The
lounge is decorated with different
themes in certain areas, a patio and
of course a welcoming bar. As well
as the fine range of real ales, there
is an excellent selection of malt
whiskys.

Plough and Harrow

107 Worcester Street, DY8 1AX

On A451 at junction of Heath Lane
B4186, opp. park.

☉ 12:00-14:30, 18:00-23:00 Mon-Fri;
12:00-23:00 Sat; 12:00-15:30, 19:00-
23:00 Sun

☎ (01384) 397218

www.ploughandharrow.net

**Enville White; Greene King IPA;
Marston's Pedigree; guest beer**

A ten minute walk from
Stourbridge Junction station or
the bus station, this smart street
front pub has no car park but there
is ample on-street parking and is
close to Mary Stevens Park (beware
- car park here is locked at night).
The single room bar has plenty of
nooks and crannies if you fancy a
quiet pint. The old brew house has
not been used for many years, but
there are always four real ales inc
an ever changing guest (known as
the 'middle wicket'). Good quality
meals including veggie choices and

roasts are served Wed-Sun (not Sun eve); snacks including rolls are available at other times. The pub boasts a nice garden for outdoor quaffing. Former Stourbridge CAMRA Pub Of The Year.

🏨Q❀◗○≹(Stourbridge Junction)

Stourbridge: Oldswinford

Shrubbery Cottage

28 Heath Lane, DY8 1RQ

Just off Oldswinford lights, towards Norton.

⊙ 12:00-23:00 Mon-Sun

☎ (01384) 377598

www.holdensbrewery.co.uk

Holden's Mild, Bitter, Special, Golden Glow, seasonal ales

Close to Stourbridge Junction railway station, this pub has been recently refurbished and is fully accessible for wheelchair users. The single room with a horseshoe shaped bar has an area with plasma TV showing sports, and a quieter lounge area.

❀ ♿ P ≹(Stourbridge Junction)

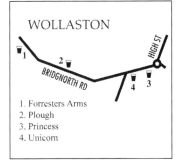

WOLLASTON

BRIDGNORTH RD

HIGH ST

1. Forresters Arms
2. Plough
3. Princess
4. Unicorn

Stourbridge: Wollaston

Forresters Arms

Bridgnorth Road, Wollaston, DY8 3PL

On A458 towards Bridgnorth

⊙ 12:00-14:30, 18:00-23:00 Mon-Sat; 12:00-14:30, 19:00-22:30 Sun

☎ (01384) 394476

Enville Ale; Marston's Pedigree; guest beers

This friendly local is well known for good value food. The T-shaped room conveniently provides a no smoking area for diners (no meals served Sun eve or Mon eve). As well as being home to the Forresters Golf Society, the pub holds regular quizzes, usually on the first and third Sunday of the month. There is also the annual fun-run for charity - an event not to be missed.
Meals served 12-2, 6.30-9 (no meals Sun eve or Mon eve).

🏨❀◗♣P

Plough

154 Bridgnorth Road, DY8 3PD

⊙ 12:00-14:30, 18:00-23:00 Mon-Fri; 12:00-16:00, 18:00-23:00 Sat; 12:00-22:30 Sun

☎ (01384) 393414

Caledonian Deuchars IPA; Coors Hancocks HB; Marston's Pedigree

This two-roomed former coaching house has a bar where cards and darts are played. The pool table is situated in an alcove off the bar while the garden features a petanque piste. An upstairs function room is also available. Diners are well catered for with a selection of good quality and good value food.

🏨❀◗⊟♣P

Princess

115-117 Bridgnorth Road, DY8 3NX

⏱ 11:00-23:00 Mon-Sat; 11:00-22:30 Sun

☎ (01384) 443687

Banks's Original; Caledonian Deuchars IPA; Greene King IPA; Wells Bombardier; guest beers

Popular community local situated in a pleasant shopping area. The pub has one large room divided into separate areas - floor boards, flag stones and carpeted areas are all to be found. A wide range of bric-a-brac adorns the walls and ceilings. A patio is available for outdoor drinking.

❀P

Unicorn

145 Bridgnorth Road, DY8 3NX

Just past Wollaston island towards Stourton.

⏱ 12:00-23:00 Mon-Sat; 12:00-16:00, 19:00-22:30 Sun

☎ (01384) 394823

Batham's Mild, Best Bitter, XXX (Winter)

Former brewhouse was purchased by Bathams in 1993 and has earned a reputation for serving one of the best pints in the estate. The old brewhouse still exists but is sadly no longer in use. The pub itself is a traditional two-roomed drinkers house appealing to all ages. Sandwiches usually available to order. Public car park behind the pub.

Q❀⛁♿P⊗

Rear of ex-Stuart Crystal factory

Tipton

Before the discovery of coal beneath its surface, Tipton was an area of meadow, pasture, woodland and heath. During the civil war it was the scene of a battle, popularly known as the Battle of Tipton Green, when Parliamentary forces unsuccessfully attempted to take Dudley Castle. The iron industry developed early in Tipton and it was at the works of the Horseley Iron Company that the first iron steamship, the Aaron Manby, was built in 1821. With the growth of industry a complex network of canals came into being, and Tipton came to be known as 'the Venice of the Midlands'. Traditional canal bridges of the Black Country were also a product of the Horseley Works. Tipton's most famous son was William Perry, the 'Tipton Slasher', champion prizefighter of England between 1850 and 1857.

Tipton: Great Bridge

Rising Sun
116 Horseley Road, DY4 7NH
Off B4517 (A461)

☼ 12:00-14:30, 17:00-23:00 Mon-Fri; 12:00-23:00 Sat; 12:00-22:30 Sun

☎ (0121) 530 2308
www.therisingsunpub.com
Banks's Original; Oakham JHB; 4 ever-changing guest beers
Victorian hostelry, retaining two distinct rooms. The bright bar, adorned with pictures of local sporting heroes, is warmed by a log-burning stove. Two open fires provide a similar function in the comfortable lounge. In summer the back yard opens for drinking and occasional functions. The pub is 10 minute walk from Great Bridge bus station, with frequent services to Dudley, West Bromwich and Birmingham. Weekday lunches are served.

🏨🌸🍴🏠♣

Tipton: Ocker Hill

Waggon & Horses
131 Toll End Road, DY4 0ET
A461

☼ 17:00-23:00 Mon-Thu; 12:00-23:00 Fri-Sat; 12:00-15:30, 19:00-22:30 Sun

☎ (0121) 502 6453
Banks's Original; Burton Bridge Stairway to Heaven; Olde Swan Entire; Stones Bitter; Toll End beers; guest beers.
Mock-tudor building with Toll End brewery at the rear. The large, busy public bar, with darts and a real fire, has an open-plan feel. The spacious, comfortable lounge displays a collection of Burton Bridge monthly beer cards. At the rear is a conservatory and landscaped garden providing a peaceful drinking area. Guest beers are usually from micro-breweries. Food is limited to summer barbecues and rolls. Buses from Dudley/Walsall: 311, 312 stop in Powis Avenue/Toll End Road; 313 stops in Leabrook Road.

🏨🌸🍴🏠⛵♣🌸⊖(Wednesbury Parkway)

Walsall

Walsall has been called "The Town of 100 Trades", and the surrounding towns that make up the modern Borough each seem to have grown from their own industrial speciality.

Walsall itself is known worldwide for the manufacture of leather goods: saddles, harnesses, etc., and has a museum dedicated to the industry housed in a former leather factory. The old town centre was from St. Matthew's church down to the Bridge, where the market has existed since the 13th Century. At the other end of the modern centre stands the award-winning New Art Gallery, built in 2000.

Walsall Arboretum originally opened in 1874, and today covers some 33 acres of trees, boating lakes and gardens. The Walsall Illuminations take place in the Arboretum every September and October; some say providing a more interesting display than those in Blackpool.

Walsall

Arbor Lights
128 Lichfield Street, WS1 1SY

🕐 10:00-23:00 Mon-Sat; 12:00-22:30 Sun

☎ (01922) 613361
Beer range varies
One room pub separated into two sections. Left hand side of pub is the drinking area, right hand side is mainly for food. Name derives from the annual illuminations held at the nearby Arboretum. Ten minutes walk from bus and rail stations.

Fountain
49 Lower Forster Street, WS1 1XB

🕐 12:00-23:00 Mon-Sat; 12:00-22:30 Sun

☎ (01922) 629741
Caledonian Deuchars IPA; Fuller's London Pride
Very popular pub just off the town centre. Two roomed pub where the lounge used to be part of a

doctors surgery. Decorated with photographs of old Walsall and old pubs. Close to Walsall Arboretum.

King George V
Wallows Lane, WS2 9BZ

🕐 11:00-23:00 Mon-Fri; 12:00-23:00 Sat; 12:00-22:30 Sun

☎ (01922) 626130
Beer range varies
Large imposing three-roomed pub. There is a lounge, games room and large function room. Built in 1936 by M&B in Art Deco Style. Games room contains a fascinating display of pub games from years gone by.

(Bescot)

Lyndon House Hotel
9/10 Upper Rushall Street, WS1 2HA
Top of Walsall Market

🕐 11:30-23:00 Mon-Sat; 12:00-22:30 Sun

☎ (01922) 612511
Courage Directors; Theakstons Mild, Bitter; House Special Bitter, Two guest beers

A bit like the Tardis. A small attractive flower-hung frontage fronts a large very comfortable one room lounge bar and a complete hotel. The complex also contains an Italian restaurant. Convenient for Walsall Market.

🏨Q✿🍴(€⇄

Prince
239 Stafford Street, WS2 8DJ

🕐 10:30-01:00 Mon-Sat; 10:30-12:00 Sun

☎ (01922) 641292

Banks's Original, Bitter; guest beer

Known as the Blucher, the pub was formerly the Prince Blucher named after the Prussian general. This two-roomed town pub attracts both local and passing trade. Always a friendly atmosphere. Exhibit your talents in the weekend karaoke nights. Pool table in the back room.

✿⌨♣P⇄

Red Lion
69 Park Street, WS1 1NW

🕐 09:00-23:00 Mon-Wed; 09:00-00:00 Thu; 09:00-01:00 Fri-Sat; 12:00-22:30 Sun

☎ (01922) 622380

Banks's Bitter; guest beer

Town centre pub close to both bus and rail stations. Handy for the art gallery. Built in 1815 but much altered, there are two rooms, with the smaller upstairs accessed by a spiral staircase. The fine late Victorian frontage is listed. Regular quiz and theme nights. Occasional guest beer.

✿(€⇄

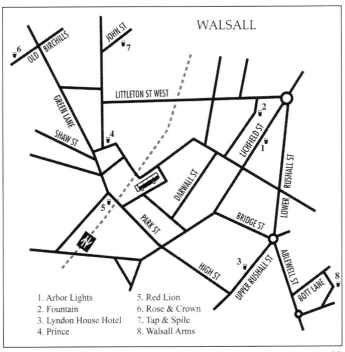

WALSALL

1. Arbor Lights
2. Fountain
3. Lyndon House Hotel
4. Prince
5. Red Lion
6. Rose & Crown
7. Tap & Spile
8. Walsall Arms

St Mathew's church

Rose & Crown

55 Old Birchills, WS2 8QH

☉ 10:00-01:00 Mon-Sun

☎ (01922) 720533

Black Country Pig On The Wall; guest beers

Expect a friendly welcome in this thriving grade II listed, three roomed corner pub dating from 1901. Guest beers are from independent breweries and there is a real cider. Live entertainment Saturday night, Karaoke Friday night and Sunday Afternoon. Sunday night quizzes. Function room available.

🏚🐕⌨♣♠

Tap & Spile

5 John Street, WS2 8AF

☉ 12:00-15:00, 18:00-23:00 Mon-Thu, Sat; 12:00-23:00 Fri; 12:00-15:00, 19:00-22:30 Sun

☎ (01922) 627660

Oakham JHB; Up to 7 guest beers

Cosy, traditional back street local. Two rooms and a corridor drinking area. Lovely old blue brick yard. One of a handful of pubs which launched CAMRA in 1972. Always known as the Pretty Bricks because of the glazed bricks on frontage. Extensive menu of outstanding quality pub food. No less than Delia Smith has praised the chips here.

🏚Q❄◗⌨♣♠

Village Pub

**Village Hotel & Leisure, Tempus
Drive, Tempus 10 Walsall, WS2 8TJ**
Adjacent to M6 Jc 10

☼ 11:00-23:00 Mon-Sat; 12:00-22:30
Sun

☎ (01922) 663661
www.villagehotelsonline.co.uk
Draught Bass; guest beer
Hotel Bar that is run as a pub,
creating a good mix of locals
and guests. There's something
different every night including
live entertainment, world cuisine,
karaoke and quizzes. Charity events
throughout the year.
⌂❶♿P☺

Walsall Arms

17 Bank Street, WS1 2EP
Behind Royal Hotel

☼ 12:00-14:00, 17:30-23:00 Mon-Fri;
12:00-15:00, 17:30-23:00 Sat; 12:00-
17:30, 19:00-22:30 Sun

☎ (01922) 725848
**Mansfield Dark Mild, Mansfield
Cask; Marston's Burton Bitter,
Pedigree; guest beer**
Traditional cheery little refuge
from the madness of the nearby
town centre circuit palaces. Cosy
smokeroom, nice little bar and
corridor drinking area. Well known
for its fine skittle alley.
Q❀⊞♣

Walsall Cricket Club

Gorway Road, WS1 3BE
Off A34, by university campus

☼ 20:00-23:00 Mon-Fri; 12:00-23:00
Sat; 12:00-22:30 Sun

☎ (01922) 622094
www.walsallcricketclub.co.uk
Marston's Burton Bitter; guest beers
Comfortable lounge with friendly
atmosphere. Bar is manned by
members themselves. A lovely

green location in town to sit inside
or out. Enjoy a match or just relax.
Regular Beer Festivals are held.
Entry to the club for non-members
is by showing this guide or a
current CAMRA card.
❀♣P

Walsall Rugby Club

Delves Road, WS1 3JY
Off A4148, By University Campus

☼ 19:00-23:00 Mon-Fri (Closed Wed);

12:00-23:00 Sat; 12:00-19:00 Sun

☎ (01922) 626818
www.walsallrufc.co.uk
**Adnams Bitter; Fuller's London
Pride; Greene King IPA, Abbot Ale;
guest beer**
The club was founded in 1922.
The large and comfortable lounge
bar occupies the shell of an old
wartime building. A popular venue
for private functions. 19 seasons of
league rugby have been played here.
Entry to the club for non-members
is by showing this guide or a
current CAMRA card.
❀♣P

White Lion

150 Sandwell Street, WS1 3EQ

☼ 12:00-23:00 Mon-Sat; 12:00-22:30
Sun

☎ (01922) 628542
**Adnams Bittter; Greene King IPA;
Old Speckled Hen; Highgate Dark;
Hook Norton Old Hooky; guest
beer**
Large imposing Edwardian back
street local. The L-shaped bar with
famous "Queasy" sloping floor is
often a lively cosmopolitan mix.
There is also a pool room and a
plush lounge. A great community
pub.
Q❀⊞♣❀

Brewing in the Borough of Walsall

Before the introduction of the 1872 Licensing Act, many pubs were brewing on the premises for their customers. The act regulated the pubs into Beerhouses or Public Houses with a full Licence (this usually meant they could also sell Wines & Spirits). With little or no transport available specially to the working man, people used to live, work and play in the same area. The local Beerhouse therefore had a ready supply of regular customers. As some of the smaller breweries closed others saw an opportunity to brew more beer and sell it to pubs nearby. Below is a sample of some of the brewing companies which evolved.

Highgate Brewery, Sandymount Road, Walsall:

Now the only active brewery in Walsall and currently owned by Aston Manor Birmingham. It was built in 1898 and supplied pubs in the Walsall area as well as acquiring its own. In 1924 it joined forces with the John Lord Town Brewery Walsall to form Walsall Proprietary Ltd which acquired Arthur Beebee Malt Shovel Brewery Sandwell Street Walsall and moved brewing to Highgate. Around 1939 it became prey to Mitchells & Butlers who looked at closing it down. However due to the war rationing of malt etc. was in force for each brewery so it was kept open to retain its allocation. It carried on as part of Mitchells & Butlers until 1995 when it was purchased by a management buy out.

Walsall & District Clubs Brewery, Daw End, Rushall:

Established in 1920 as Walsall District Clubs Co-operative Brewing Society, it took over the Old Rushall Brewery premises which was registered in 1905 and had ceased trading in 1915. In 1947 it changed its name to the Walsall & District Clubs Brewery. In 1961 in conjunction with Gibbs Mew of Salisbury it purchased the Lancashire Clubs Brewery of Barrowford. A new company Gibbs Keg Brewery was formed, the Rushall Brewery was sold shortly afterwards to Charrington & Company of Mile End London.

John Lord Town Brewery, Short Acre Street, Walsall:

In 1896 John Lord purchased the Black Horse Inn and land next door. By 1898 he had built a four storey brewery alongside the pub to brew his beer. He formed a partnership in 1924 with Highgate Brewery, as Walsall Proprietary Ltd. This company took over Arthur BeeBee Malt Shovel Brewery Sandwell St Walsall and closed it with brewing moving to Highgate. They carried on brewing until 1939 when they were taken over by Mitchells & Butlers and closed.

Butts Brewery, Butts Street, Walsall:

The Butts Inn brewed its own beer on the premises from at least 1896. The above company was registered in 1920 to acquire the Butts Inn its brewery and two other pubs. One of new owners was a James Bird whose family ran the Crown Brewery in Bloxwich. In 1929 the business went into voluntary liquidation and James Bird invested the money into the Crown Brewery.

N.F. Bird Crown Brewery, 6 Leamore Lane, Bloxwich:

Brewing commenced in 1864 and continued in the hands of the Bird family. In 1929 investment was made into the brewery and its pubs on the closure of the Butts Brewery . The name changed to N. F. Bird in 1960 but by 1965 it had ceased brewing. It was acquired by Ansells brewery in 1967.

Bloxwich Brewery, Elmore Green Road, Bloxwich:

Registered as a company in 1898, it clearly brewed good beer as it began to acquire many pubs in the area. The brewery was closed in 1925 and its 42 pubs purchased by Butlers.

James Pritchard & Son, Darlaston Brewery, Church Street, Darlaston:

Founded in 1896 it supplied pubs mainly in the Darlaston and Wednesbury areas, although it also had some outlets in Bilston. It continued brewing on the site until it was taken over by Butlers and closed in 1947.

Lashfords Brewery, St Annes Rd, Willenhall:

Established around 1900 by Jesse Lashford to supply the Spring Bank Tavern on the corner of St Annes Rd and Springvale Street. Things must have gone well as the New Inn, Darlaston and Prince Of Wales, Wednesbury were purchased. In the 1920's they purchased the Old Willenhall Football ground in St Anne's Road and converted it into a Greyhound track. However in 1930 they decided to sell up their property interests to Truman, Hanbury & Buxton of London and the brewery closed.

Wednesbury

Wednesbury has Saxon origins, and may have a claim to be the historic centre of the Black Country as coal was found here in the 14th Century, and mining developed here earlier than elsewhere. Later Wednesbury became the centre of the tube making industry, and was also known for the production of railway coach ironwork.

Wednesbury
Bellwether
3-4 Walsall Street, WS10 9BZ

⏰ 10:00-23:00 Mon-Sun

☎ (0121) 502 6404

Banks's Bitter; Greene King Abbot Ale; Hop Back Summer Lightning; Shepherd Neame Spitfire; guest beers

Typical Wetherspoons outlet. The Bellwether stands almost alone in offering a wide range of beers in the town centre. All ages are attracted, and it can get particularly busy on Friday and Saturday. Normal Wetherspoon beer festivals are included.

Q❀◗⅄☺

Cottage Spring
106 Franchise Street, WS10 9RG

⏰ 14:00-23:00 Mon-Thu; 12:00-23:00 Fri-Sat; 12:00-22:30 Sun

☎ (0121) 526 6254

Holden's Bitter, Golden Glow; guest beer

18th Century two room pub. Photographs of the pub from 1950s & 60s adorn the walls. Public bar features one of the early editions of Red Telephone Boxes. Conservatory at rear is used by diners.

Q❀◗⊟♣P

Old Blue Ball
19 Hall End, WS10 9ED

⏰ 12:00-15:00, 17:00-23:00 Mon-Thu; 12:00-23:00 Fri; 12:00-17:00, 19:00-23:00 Sat; 12:00-15:30, 19:00-22:30 Sun

☎ (0121) 556 0197

Everards Original; Highgate Dark; guest beers

Traditional three-roomed back street local. Bar is adorned by Mugs, Toby Jugs & chamber pots hanging from ceiling. Corridor drinking area and snugs are served via serving hatch. Large family room.

Q⅄❀⊟♣

Old Leathern Bottel
40 Vicarage Road, WS10 9DU

⏰ 12:00-14:30 (not Mon), 18:00-23:00 Mon-Fri; 12:00-23:00 Sat; 12:00-15:30, 19:00-22:30 Sun

☎ (0121) 505 0230

Greene King Ruddles County, Abbot Ale; Wells Bombardier; Worthington Cask

16th Century coaching inn that is the oldest pub in Wednesbury. The pub has a separate bar, snug and a lounge divided for drinkers and diners. Reputedly haunted building.

Q⅄❀◗⊟♣P

Porter and Stout

The origins of Porter and Stout are buried in London at the turn of the 18th Century. A popular drink at this time was called Three Threads, made by publicans mixing pale, young brown and matured stale brown ales. This was the first Porter. The London brewers, due to their cramped sites, had no choice but to buy in expensive pale and stale beers from the country for this. They developed a London style of Porter known as Entire Butt, or just Entire, which was made as a single brew and much cheaper to produce. Both Three Threads and Entire gained the nickname Porter, with the two styles surviving side by side for much of the 18th Century. The name Porter is said to have come from the beer's popularity with London's Porters of that era, but there are also other theories.

In 1788 Porter reached Bristol; in 1796 it was exported to Russia, and had also reached Scotland. Stout had also appeared, which to start was a stronger or 'stouter' Porter. By this time all Porter and Stout was made as Entire, but the end was in sight: Porters and Stouts took months to condition, unlike Milds and Pale Ales which were known as "running beers", because they only took a few days to condition, before leaving the brewery. By the mid 19th century, many breweries had ripped out their deep fermentation vats for shallower ones to make more of the running beers, and Porter and Stout were in terminal decline. The First World War hit the final blow from which Porter and Stout could not recover, except in Ireland where they still flourished.

Today however, Porters and Stouts are enjoying a revival. One of the biggest brand names, Guinness, is still very popular, but as it is pasteurised, filtered and chilled, it is not what it once was. The revival of Cask Conditioned Stout and Porter was helped by Whitbread brewing a Porter to celebrate its 250th anniversary in 1992. Other smaller brewers followed suit and were surprised by the popularity.

Today, Stouts and Porters tend to get lumped together as a category, but in reality there are differences between the two styles. Unfortunately, a lot of brewers don't seem to know the difference and some beers that are called Stouts are really Porters and vice versa. Stouts should get their bitterness and darkness through the use of roasted malt and barley, whereas Porters should be more obviously hopped with their darkness coming from black malt.

Whatever they are called they make a very tasty alternative to bitters, so give one a try and sample some history in a glass.

For further information, see CAMRA's "Homebrew Classics Stout & Porter" book by Clive La Pensee and Roger Protz.

Wednesfield

The first record of Wednesfield was in 910 when a battle took place between the Saxons and Danes. Its name is of Pagan Saxon origin from 'Woden'. This sleepy mainly rural hamlet remained relatively undeveloped well into the 20th Century. It gained its own church and became a parish in its own right, but by 1891 its population was still only 5000.

The trades were varied and mainly small scale: locks, keys, traps and latches, etc. Nearby Heath Town part of the parish had more people and had started to become industrialised with some factories and a growth in housing. The lack of development means that some of its old pubs have survived and are still open today.

The Dog & Partridge built around 1818 and the Boat built around 1860 both brewed their own beer, and both are grade two listed (including the Boat's brewery building). The splendid traditional Pyle Cock built in 1867 is the last old building left in Rookery Street. With the need for even more housing, Wolverhampton began encroaching into Wednesfield and by 1966 it had been absorbed into Wolverhampton.

Wednesfield
Dog & Partridge
High Street, WV11 1SZ

🕐 11:00-23:00 Mon-Sat; 12:00-22:30 Sun

☎ (01902) 723490

Banks's Original, Bitter; guest beer
A listed building circa 1818 has been opened out, altered and extended over the years. However, with its wooden beams and original cooking range retained, you still get a sense of its age. Its original well was rediscovered and incorporated in the rear extension. Bus 559 stops nearby.
🏘🌸◖P

Pyle Cock
Rookery Street, WV11 1UN
(On old Wolverhampton road)

🕐 10:30-23:00 Mon-Sat; 12:00-22:30 Sun

☎ (01902) 732125

Banks's Original, Bitter; guest beers
A superb small pub dating back to around 1865 which offers a bar, smoke room and rear lounge. It attracts a wide mix of regulars and offers a warm welcome to all visitors. The landlord was awarded a CAMRA mild merit award in 2005. Visit and enjoy. Bus 559 stops nearby.
🌸◖P

Royal Tiger

41-43 High Street, WV11 1ST

🕐 09:00-00:00 Sun-Thu; 09:00-01:00 Fri-Sat

☎ (01902) 307816

Greene King Abbot Ale; Marston's Burton Bitter; guest beers

A purpose built Wetherspoons pub, opened on the site of the former Domes bakery. It extends back from the entrance and provides a patio alongside the canal at the rear. The building to its right, part occupied by the bookmakers, was the original Royal Tiger closed in 1994. 559 bus stops outside.

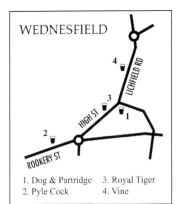

WEDNESFIELD

1. Dog & Partridge   3. Royal Tiger
2. Pyle Cock   4. Vine

Vine

35 Lichfield Road, WV11 1TW

🕐 12:00-15:00, 19:00-23:00 Mon-Sat; 12:00-15:00, 19:00-22:30 Sun - May alter lunchtimes

☎ (01902) 733529

Everards Beacon; guest beers

Built in 1938, to replace the original, it is a rare example of an inter-war pub. On CAMRA National Inventory of pub interiors and grade II listed. With a choice of three rooms, it is a treat to sit in the bar in front of a roaring fire, drinking a pint of real ale. Bus 559 stops outside.

♨⊟P

West Bromwich

The original village of West Bromwich was to the north of the present town centre. Enclosure of common lands in the early 19th century brought about the development of the high street which had previously been little more than a track across an area of open heathland. Industrial development took place rather later than in other Black Country towns and West Bromwich became noted for a diversity of products ranging from spring balances to motor vehicles. West Bromwich Albion Football Club began as a works team of the Salter company. West Bromwich can boast a number of historic buildings including the medieval Manor House, the earliest part of which dates from the late 13th century, and the Oak House, a timber-framed Tudor building.

West Bromwich: Carters Green

Old Crown

56 Sandwell Road, B70 8TJ
200 yards off High Street which is off A41/A4035

☉ 12:00-16:00, 17:00-23:00 Mon-Fri; 12:00-23:00 Sat; 12:00-3:30, 19:00-22:30 Sun

☎ (0121) 525 4600
Up to 4 ever-changing guest beers
Popular back-street free-house with a varied clientele. It is renowned for its home-made curries and baltis which are served lunchtimes Mon-Fri and evenings Tue-Fri. 10 minute walk from West Bromwich town centre. Buses from Dudley/Birmingham: 74; from Wednesbury/Birmingham: 78; from Wolverhampton/Birmingham: 79. Metro stop: Dartmouth Street then a 5 minute walk.
◑♣⊖(Dartmouth Street)

Wheatsheaf

379 High Street, B70 9QW
Off A41/A4035

☉ 11:00-23:00 Sun-Thu; 11:00-23:30 Fri-Sat

☎ (0121) 553 4221
Holden's Mild, Bitter, Golden Glow, seasonal beers
Behind the handsome frontage is a long front bar, comfortable lounge and rear patio. Classic pub food is served, including 'doorstop' roast pork sandwiches. It can be very busy on WBA match days, when traditional Black Country dishes of faggots & peas and 'gray paes' & bacon are served. The cider is Thatcher's Cheddar Valley. 10 minute walk from West Bromwich town centre. Buses from Dudley/Birmingham: 74; from Wednesbury/Birmingham: 78; from Wolverhampton/Birmingham: 79. Metro stops: Dartmouth Street then a 5 minute walk; Dudley Street Guns Village then a 5 minute walk past the clock tower into Carters Green.
❂◑⊞♣♥⊖(Dartmouth Street/ Guns Village)

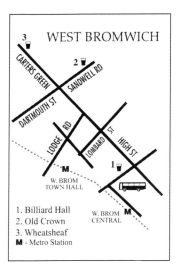

WEST BROMWICH

3
2
1

CARTERS GREEN
SANDWELL RD
DARTMOUTH ST
LODGE RD
LOMBARD ST
HIGH ST

M
W. BROM
TOWN HALL

W. BROM
CENTRAL
M

1. Billiard Hall
2. Old Crown
3. Wheatsheaf
M - Metro Station

West Bromwich: Churchfields

Churchfield Tavern
18 Little Lane, B71 4HR

🕐 11:00-23:00 Mon-Sat; 12:00-22:30 Sun

☎ (0121) 588 5468
Banks's Original, Bitter
Traditional back street pub opposite Sandwell Hospital A&E Dept. Public bar at front with quarry tiled floor. Corridor leads to two comfortable lounges and a conservatory. These get very busy at lunch times with hospital staff. Conservatory overlooks a seated garden area. The pub also has its own bowling green.

Horse and Jockey
49 Stoney Lane, B71 4EZ

🕐 11:00-23:00 Mon-Sat; 11:00-23:30 Sun

☎ (0121) 553 7003
Banks's Original, Bitter
In this popular back street pub, the public bar at the front caters for the usual pub games. The two lounges (one is non smoking) at the rear get very busy at weekends with live entertainment. There is also a conservatory containing a pool table.

Jolly Nailor
28 Lyndon, B71 4EJ
At rear of Sandwell Hospital

🕐 12:00-23:00 Mon-Fri; 11:00-23:00 Sat; 12:00-22:30 Sun

☎ (0121) 601 2505
Banks's Original, Bitter
Small friendly three-roomed back street pub. Leading from the front entrance is a small but comfortable snug. The public bar has the usual pub games. The former lounge at the rear is now a pool room.

Royal Oak
14 Newton Street, B71 3RQ

🕐 15:00-23:00 Mon-Fri; 12:00-23:00 Sat-Sun

☎ (0121) 588 7570
Beer range varies
Built in 1830's, this popular pint sized pub has two rooms. Built on fork of two side roads with small bar. Very popular on match days with WBA fans. Comfortable lounge at rear that attracts all ages. Parking is difficult.

West Bromwich: Kenrick Park

Vine

152 Roebuck Street, B70 6RD
By M5 junction 1

☼ 11:00-14:30, 17:00-23:00 Mon-Thu; 11:30-23:00 Fri; 12:00-23:00 Sat; 12:00-22:30 Sun

☎ (0121) 553 2866

1 ever-changing guest beer

This pub looks like a traditional corner local from the outside but has a tardis-like interior: a tiny snug, smoke room and a back bar opening out into a large glass-roofed extension, with further dining room beyond and access to a marquee including children's play area. It is famous for its curries and spectacular indoor Indian barbecue. 10 minute walk from West Bromwich town centre. Buses from Dudley/Birmingham: 74; from Wednesbury/Birmingham: 78; from Wolverhampton/Birmingham: 79. Metro stop: Kenrick Park then a 5 minute walk towards the motorway bridge and follow the footpath alongside it. Railway Station: Smethwick Galton Bridge then a complicated 10 minute walk.

◑ ⊟⇌(Smethwick Galton Bridge) ⊖(Kenrick Park)

West Bromwich: Town Centre

Billiard Hall

St Michael's Ringway, B70 7AB
Off High Street, opposite bus station

☼ 09:00-00:00 Sun-Thu; 09:00-01:00 Fri-Sat

☎ (0121) 580 2892

Highgate Dark Mild; Hop Back Summer Lightning; Greene King Abbot Ale; Marston's Burton Bitter, Pedigree; guest beers

Wetherspoon conversion. This single-storey building, with its striking stone relief pediment, stands on the ring road which surrounds the shopping area. The décor is spotty, in keeping with the building's past. There is a sound-free sports screen. Food served until 11pm.

◑ ♥⊗⊖(West Bromwich Central)

Oak House

Willenhall

Willenhall was a Royal Manor at the time of the Domesday Book, owned by the King. By the 19th Century its nickname was "Umpshire" due to the stoop working men developed from the manual labour involved in the manufacture of locks. A former locksmith's workshop has been converted into the Lock Museum.

Willenhall
Cross Keys
32 Ashmore Lane Road, WV12 4LB

🕐 12:00-23:00 Mon-Sat; 12:00-22:30 Sun

☎ (01902) 411128

Banks's Original; Greene King Abbot Ale

Large single-roomed pub served by a central bar. Attracts a varied clientele. Families are very welcome. There is a bouncy castle in the garden during the summer. Pool Table.

❀◖ P ⊗

Falcon
77 Gomer Street West, WV13 2NR

🕐 12:00-23:00 Mon-Sat; 12:00-22:30 Sun

☎ (01902) 633378

Greene King Abbot Ale; Oakham JHB; Olde Swan Dark Swan; RCH Pitchfork; guest beers

The Falcon has, for several years been the flagship real ale pub in Willenhall. A genuine freehouse only a short walk from the town centre with up to eight cask beers available. Originally built in 1936, this two-roomed pub is welcoming to all and popular with the local community. The lively bar is countered by a quieter rear lounge.

Q⊟♣

Malthouse
The Dale, New Road, WV13 2BG

🕐 09:00-00:00 Mon-Thu; 09:00-01:00 Fri-Sat; 09:00-00:00 Sun

☎ (01902) 635273

Enville Ale; Greene King Abbot Ale; Marston's Burton Bitter, Pedigree; guest beers

As the name suggests, this Wetherspoons started life as a malthouse, becoming a cinema and then a bingo hall before converting into today's popular pub. The usual promotions, twice yearly-beer festivals & clubs (Curry, Steak & Chinese) etc.

❀◖♿⊗

Robin Hood
54 The Crescent, WV13 2QR

🕐 12:00-15:00, 17:00-23:00 Mon-Fri; 12:00-15:00, 19:00-23:00 Sat; 12:00-15:00 19:00-22:30 Sun

☎ (01902) 608006

Fuller's London Pride; Shepherd Neame Spitfire; Taylor Landlord; Tetley Bitter, Burton Ale

Small friendly pub with single U-shaped room where you will soon feel at home. The mainly local trade support charity events throughout the year. A local archery club meets at the weekends, practising in the adjacent field. Quiz night every 2nd Monday.

❀P

Wolverhampton

Wolverhampton was granted city status in 2000 which completed its journey from a hamlet built on land donated by Lady Wulfruna in 996 AD into a village then a town.

In 1848 it was granted its Charter of Incorporation into a self-controlling borough and the first elections were held. At the core of the centre is St Peter's Church built in 1210 as a replacement for the previous Collegiate Church it became St Peter's in 1258. The oldest building in Wolverhampton has overseen the city's growth and alterations ever since. These included in 1512 the Grammar School, 1794 Town Library and 1825 horse racing being established. By 1831 the population had reached 24,732: however just a year later this number was greatly reduced as the town was hit by a Cholera epidemic.

As the industrial revolution gathered pace, it saw a large influx of people: many of them were housed in poorly built and cramped courts (flats) near to their work places. At the same time many beer houses sprang up to satisfy the thirst of the new workers. In 1866 Queen Victoria visited the town, followed in 1869 by a grand exhibition at the Molineux Grounds, now the home of Wolverhampton Wanderers Football Club. The splendid grade II listed Molineux Hotel (House) which has been derelict for years and subject to a severe fire in 2003 is close to being fully restored.

In 1871 the splendid new town hall (now the Magistrates Courts) was built and it was from here that the first major redevelopment of the town in the 1880s was administered. This development of the Lichfield Street area saw the loss of 20 pubs: out of the ruins rose the splendid Posada Inn and in 1885 the Art Gallery. In 1895 the town was first lighted by electricity: the motto 'Out of Darkness Cometh Light' is featured on the City's Coat of Arms.

By the turn of the century Wolverhampton already had two major railway stations and an extensive steam and horse drawn tram network across the town. In 1902 the council took the bold decision to 'Go Electric' and installed the Lorain tram system, the only town to do so. Unlike other systems the electric power came from underneath rather than overhead: it operated successfully for 20 years. Around the same time regular bus services also began.

Another first for the town was the installation of Britain's first traffic lights in Lichfield Street in 1927. Wolverhampton produced bicycles, motor cycles, motor cars (Sunbeam and Star) and is also famous for its Chubb locks and safes, who opened their purpose-built trianglular building in 1898 in Fryer Street which now has a variety of uses.

The early 1960's saw the building of the Mander and Wulfrun shopping centres with the loss of several pubs including two old coaching inns. The current plans for regeneration will see a new major shopping complex (New Summer Row) and mixed use development of both the Low Level Railway Station and Springfield Brewery site. With its friendly multicultural mix, variety of pubs and attractions, visitors are assured of a pleasant experience.

Wolverhampton: Bradmore

Gunmakers Arms

63 Trysull Road, WV3 7JE
Approx 2 miles SW of city centre
🕐 11:30-23:00 Mon-Sat; 12:00-22:30 Sun

☎ (01902) 331414
Banks's Original, Bitter
Large Banks's community pub, with customers both young and more mature. The pub has a large bar and a separate lounge room. The ale is always well kept and the lunchtime menu very tasty, with the emphasis on value for money. Various entertainments include Monday night quizzes, karaoke on a Wednesday and discos on Fridays. TV sport is shown on a large screen, while pool, darts and dominoes are played by the bar regulars. Buses 513, 514A & 514C stop nearby.
●◖⊞♣P

Wolverhampton: Castlecroft

Firs

Windmill Lane, WV3 8HG
🕐 11:30-23:00 Mon-Tue; 11:30-23:30 Wed-Thu; 11:30-00:00 Fri-Sat; 12:00-23:00 Sun

☎ (01902) 763036
Banks's Original, Bitter
Large community pub, well known for its charity events. The bar has a pool table and TV screen showing Sky sports. Meals are served in the lounge until 8pm. 543 bus stops nearby.
●◖⊞P☺

Prince Albert's statue, Queen Square

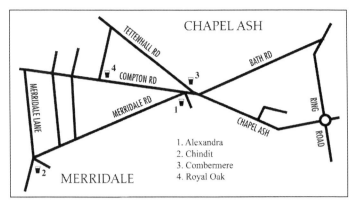

1. Alexandra
2. Chindit
3. Combermere
4. Royal Oak

Wolverhampton: Chapel Ash

Alexandra

33 Clifton Street, WV3 0QT
At A41/A454 Junction

🕐 11:00-23:00 Mon-Sat; 12:00-22:30 Sun

☎ (01902) 712416
Banks's Original; Wadworth 6X; guest beer

Although essentially a one room pub, the split bar effectively creates two drinking areas, as well as an area dominated by the pool table. The customers of this traditional community pub are a varied and characterful bunch. The pub hosts a DJ on Friday nights, and live music Saturdays and Sundays. The pub is now established on the Chapel Ash drinking circuit. Buses 501, 510, 513 & 543 stop nearby.

Combermere Arms

90 Chapel Ash, WV3 0TY
at A41/A454 jct

🕐 11:00-15:00, 17:30-23:00 Mon-Thu; 12:00-23:00 Fri-Sat; 12:00-22:30 Sun

☎ (01902) 421880
Banks's Original, Bitter; guest beers

This small, terraced pub with five separate, but very intimate, drinking areas: a bar, smoke room, family room, corridor and covered courtyard. A beer garden is also used for summer drinking. The pub is particularly busy at weekends and when Wolves are at home. The pub is named after Viscount Combermere, Wellington's cavalry commander in the Peninsular war. Gentlemen can enjoy the company of a tree in the toilets. Buses 501, 510, 513 & 543 stop nearby.

Royal Oak

70 Compton Road, WV3 9PH
On A454 1 mile from city centre

🕐 11:00-23:00 Mon-Sat; 12:00-22:30 Sun

☎ (01902) 422845
Banks's Bitter; guest beer

This 19th century managed Banks's pub is set on a main road and provides a warm welcome. Music played by a DJ is the entertainment on Thursday and Saturday evenings. Quizzes are held on Sunday evenings. The heated outdoor patio drinking area is also popular at this extended one room pub. On 510 bus route.

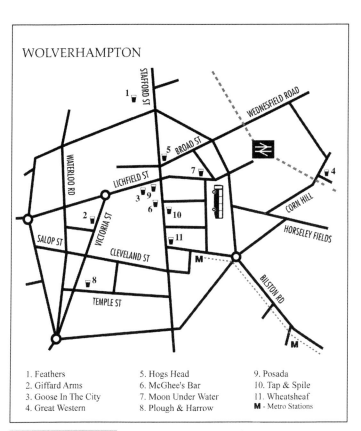

WOLVERHAMPTON

1. Feathers
2. Giffard Arms
3. Goose In The City
4. Great Western

5. Hogs Head
6. McGhee's Bar
7. Moon Under Water
8. Plough & Harrow

9. Posada
10. Tap & Spile
11. Wheatsheaf
M - Metro Stations

Wolverhampton: City Centre

Feathers

Molineux Street, WV1 1RY

🕐 12:00-23:00 Mon-Sat; 12:00-22:30 Sun

☎ (01902) 426924

Banks's Original, Bitter

Built in 1909, the Feathers holds the longest continuous licence in the city. It tends to be crowded on match days as it is opposite the Steve Bull stand of the football ground. In the heart of the university campus, it is used by locals, students and university staff who work opposite. Lunches served Monday to Saturday.

🌑◖⌂♣

Giffard Arms

64 Victoria Street, WV1 3NX

🕐 11:00-23:00 Mon-Wed; 11:00-01:00 Thu; 11:00-02:00 Fri-Sat; 12:00-22:30 Sun

☎ (01902) 426664

Wells Bombardier; Wychwood Hobgoblin; guest beer

This city-centre pub is popular mainly with goths and rockers, but don't let this put you off as this is a friendly pub which can have a mixed crowd. The interior is unique and unusual consisting of coffin-shaped tables, wall-mounted demons as well as a wooden carved throne in the middle of the room. Can be noisy during the evenings due to the loud music!

St Peter's Church

Goose in the City
32-36 Lichfield Street, WV1 1DN

🕐 11:00-23:00 Mon-Sat; 12:00-22:30 Sun

☎ (01902) 717843

Brains SA; Marston's Pedigree; Wells Bombardier; guest beers

Converted from two shops, the Goose is a large open-plan pub opposite the city's art gallery. The five real ales and food (served all day) are served at competitive prices. It is a popular pre-clubbing venue at weekends. Very convenient for a number of city centre bus-stops.

◑ ♿ ⊗ ⇄ ⊖ (St George's)

Great Western
Sun Street, WV10 0DJ

🕐 11:00-23:00 Mon-Sat; 12:00-15:00, 19:00-22:30 Sun

☎ (01902) 351090

Batham's Best Bitter; Holden's Mild, Bitter, Golden Glow, Special; guest beers

The Western is more than a good pub, it is a local icon. Built in 1869 opposite the GWR station, it has a well deserved reputation for the

standard of its cask ales and good quality home made food. A pub well loved by locals and visitors alike: a must if you are near the rail station.

❀ ◑ ♿ ♣ P ⇄

Hog's Head
186 Stafford Street, WV1 1NA

🕐 12:00-23:00 Mon-Thu; 12:00-00:00 Fri-Sat; 12:00-23:30 Sun

☎ (01902) 717955

Caledonian Deuchars IPA; Enville White; Greene King Old Speckled Hen; Wells Bombardier; Young's Bitter; guest beers

Built around 1889 as the Vine (the name is still evident in the brickwork), it closed in 1984 before reopening as the Hogshead in 1998. TV screens showing various sports, two pool tables and a bar football table mainly attract younger people in the evenings, lunchtimes are quieter. Food is served daily until 9pm.

❀ ◑ ♿ ⊗ ⇄ ⊖ (St George's)

McGhee's Bar

Wheelers Fold, WV1 1HN
off Princess Street behind Posada

☉ 10:00-23:00 Mon-Sun

☎ 07737 263669

Beer range varies

One-roomed Irish bar tucked away in an alley behind Lichfield Street. One or two ever-changing guest beers are sold, often unusual for the area. Occasional live music is staged. Five minutes walk from bus and metro stations.

⇌Θ(St George's)

Moon Under Water

53-55 Lichfield Street, WV1 1EQ
opposite Grand Theatre

☉ 09:00-00:00 Sun-Thu; 09:00-01:00 Fri-Sat

☎ (01902) 422447

Banks's Original; Greene King Abbot Ale; Marston's Burton Bitter, Pedigree; guest beers

Typical open-plan Wetherspoon's offering, popular with theatre goers at the Grand Theatre, opposite. The decor includes interesting historic Wolverhampton photographs. It can be very busy on Friday and Saturday evenings. Close to both bus and rail stations.

◗ ♿ ♣ ⊗ ⇌Θ(St George's)

Plough & Harrow

17 Worcester Street, WV2 4LD

☉ 11:00-23:00 Sun-Fri; 11:00-01:00 Sat

☎ (01902) 717575

Banks's Original

This single storey pub with slated roof is one of the oldest in the city - built in the 1860's. This basic pub has wooden beams and has been opened out. It has survived several redevelopments over the years, and it is set to be retained as part of a new shopping development. Food is served 12-6 Mon, Wed-Sat; 12-2 Sun.

◖

Lady Wulfruna statue

Posada

48 Lichfield Street, WV1 1DG

☼ 12:00-23:30 Mon-Fri; 11:00-23:00 Sat; 12:00-22:30 Sun

☎ (01902) 429011

Adnams Broadside; Caledonian Deuchars IPA; Shepherd Neame Spitfire; Taylor Landlord; Tetley Mild

Grade II listed pub, built in 1875, with an imposing tiled frontage. The interior features more original tiling, a magnificent bar back and an intimate alcove. Food is served daily until 6pm.

◖➽⊖(St George's)

Tap & Spile

35 Princess Street, WV1 1HD

☼ 11:00-23:00 Mon-Sat; 12:00-22:30 Sun

☎ (01902) 713319

Banks's Bitter; guest beers

A city-centre pub consisting of three rooms, handily placed for both the bus and metro stations. An ever-changing beer selection and competitive prices make this a popular pub. Can get very busy when Wolves are at home. Westons cider stocked. Close to metro & bus stations.

❀●➽⊖(St George's)

Wheatsheaf Hotel

Market Street, WV1 3AE

Next to Police Station

☼ 11:00-23:00 Mon-Fri; 10:30-23:00 Sat; 12:00-16:00 Sun

☎ (01902) 424446

Banks's Original, Bitter

Traditional city centre pub, also offering accommodation. It has three rooms, all served from a single bar, and a conservatory. Some of the seats in the smoke room retain a bell push, although they are no longer in use.

🛏️⊞➽⊖(St George's)

108

Wolverhampton: Compton

Swan (at Compton)

Bridgnorth Road, WV6 8AE

At Compton Island

☼ 11:00-15:00, 17:00-23:00 Mon-Fri; 11:00-23:00 Sat; 12:00-22:30 Sun

☎ (01902) 754736

Banks's Original, Bitter; Marston's Pedigree

Unspoilt grade II listed inn with traditional bar having wooden settles, exposed beams and a faded painting of a swan dated from 1777. The bar and L-shaped lounge are supplied from a central servery. Bus 510 from the city stops right outside.

Q❀⊞♣P

Wolverhampton: Finchfield

Chestnut Tree

2 Castlecroft Road, WV3 8BT

at Finchfield Road West junction

☼ 12:00-23:00 Sun-Thu; 12:00-00:00 Fri-Sat

☎ (01902) 760001

Banks's Bitter; guest beer

Community pub saved from the bulldozer following a successful locals' campaign in 2005. The single room, divided into cosy alcoves, has a pool table and TV at one end, and a dining area at the other (food served 12-8). A raised patio provides a pleasant outdoor drinking area. Bus 543 from the city stops in Finchfield Road West.

❀●Pⓢ

Wolverhampton: Merridale

Chindit

113 Merridale Road, WV3 9SE

🕐 14:00-00:00 Mon-Fri; 12:00-00:00 Sat-Sun

☎ (01902) 425582

Caledonian Deuchars IPA, guest beers

Street-corner pub with a comfortable lounge and a bar with a pool table. The ever-changing selection of cask beers are always in excellent condition, earning the pub Cask Marque recognition. Live music is held on Friday evenings and a beer festival is staged over May Day weekend. Buses 513 & 543 from the city stop outside.

❀⏁P

Wolverhampton: Monmore Green

Red Lion

252 Bilston Road, WV2 2HU

🕐 12:00-23:00 Mon-Sat; 12:00-22:30 Sun

☎ (01902) 454511

Banks's Original

The only survivor of the many old pubs that were originally along Bilston Road. Relatively unaltered with its bar, small smoke room and lounge, which was originally two separate rooms. Handy for Monmore Green stadium and bus 79 stops nearby.

⏁P⊖(Priestfield)

"Lindy Lou" Victoria Street

Wolverhampton: Oxley
Homestead
Lodge Road, WV10 6TQ
Off A449 at Goodyear island

🕐 14:00-23:00 Mon-Thu; 12:00-23:00 Fri-Sat; 12:00-22:30 Sun

☎ (01902) 787357
Beer range varies

Large, two roomed pub which was originally a farmhouse. The pub consists of a sizeable bar and a comfortable lounge where home-cooked food is served (no meals Sun eve). Bus Nos 503, 504 and 506 from the city centre stop on the main Stafford Road (stop after Goodyear Island).

❀ ⮑ ◐ ⊟ ♣ P

Wolverhampton: Penn
Old Stag's Head
65 Church Hill, WV4 5JB
Next to church

🕐 11:45-14:30, 18:00-23:00 Mon-Sat; 12:00-17:00, 19:00-22:30 Sun

☎ (01902) 341023
Banks's Original, Bitter

Rustic pub on the edge of Penn Common, next to St Bartholomew's church, with a small bar and a larger lounge where children are welcome if eating. No food Sunday evening.

❀ ◐ ⊟ ♣ P

Roebuck
384 Penn Road, WV4 4DE
3 miles from city centre on A449

🕐 11:00-23:00 Mon-Sat; 11:30-22:30 Sun

☎ (01902) 331307
Banks's Original, Bitter; Marston's Pedigree

Popular Banks's pub located in a quiet area of Wolverhampton with a friendly atmosphere and

comfortable seating. Good value food available daily. Buses 256 & 260 stop nearby.

❀ ◐ ⅙ ♣ P

Wolverhampton: Tettenhall
Mitre Inn
4 Lower Green, WV6 9AH
At bottom of "Tettenhall Rock" cutting adjacent to A41

🕐 12:00-15:00; 17:30-00:00 Mon-Thu; 12:00-01:00 Fri-Sat; 12:00-22:30 Sun

☎ (01902) 567890
www.urbangastro.co.uk
Banks's Original; Greene King IPA, Old Speckled Hen

Recently revamped pub/restaurant with award-winning menu, oak bar and beams, stone floor and open fire. There is a welcoming busy feel about the whole place. Bar meals prepared with fresh produce - see chalkboard. Occasional guest cider (Addlestone's). On street parking available (one way). Bus 501 stops on The Rock.

⚲ ❀ ◐

Rock Hotel
7 Old Hill, WV6 8QB
Up Old Hill from "The Rock" Cutting (A41)

🕐 11:00-23:00 Mon-Sat; 12:00-22:30 Sun

☎ (01902) 746681
Tetley Bitter; guest beer

Large, food-orientated establishment with space mainly allocated to the dining area. The bar area is served from the main counter. The spacious garden gives an outstanding view out over Wolverhampton. Five minutes walk from 501 bus stops on A41.

⛺ ❀ ◐ ⊟ ⅙ P

Wolverhampton: Tettenhall Wood

Royal Oak
7 School Road, WV6 8EJ
Up the Holloway from Compton island (A454)

🕐 12:00-23:00 Mon-Sat; 12:00-22:30 Sun

☎ (01902) 754396

Banks's Original, Bitter

Attractive grade II listed building with cable TV and dominoes in the bar, and a cosy lounge seating just twelve. A large fenced garden contains a function room, a volleyball/five-a-side pitch and a children's play area. Bus 510 from the city stops right outside.

●◐⇲♣⊟

Shoulder of Mutton
62 Wood Road, WV6 8NF
Up the Holloway from Compton island (A454)

🕐 11:30-14:30, 17:00-23:00 (23:30 Fri); 11:30-23:30 Sat; 12:00-23:30 Sun

☎ (01902) 756672

Banks's Original, Bitter; guest beer

One-roomed low-ceilinged pub with a warm welcome assured. Good value traditional home-cooked food served lunchtime only. Occasional live entertainment on weekday evenings. Large car park and patio area with space for barbecues. Five minutes walk from 510 bus stops in Church Road (from city centre) & School Road (towards city centre).

Q●◐⇲♣P⊗

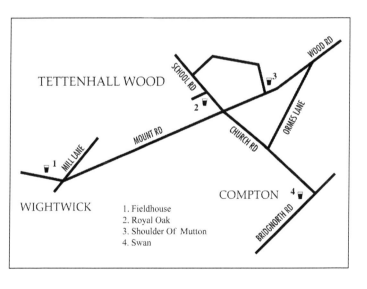

TETTENHALL WOOD

WOOD RD

SCHOOL RD

3

ORMES LANE

MOUNT RD

CHURCH RD

MILL LANE

1

WIGHTWICK

2

COMPTON

4

BRIDGNORTH RD

1. Fieldhouse
2. Royal Oak
3. Shoulder Of Mutton
4. Swan

Wolverhampton: Whitmore Reans

Newhampton Inn

19 Riches Street, WV6 0DW

🕐 11:00-23:00 Mon-Sat; 12:00-22:30 Sun

☎ (01902) 745773

Caledonian Deuchars IPA; Courage Best Bitter, Directors; Greene King Abbot Ale; Theakston Old Peculier; guest beer

Street corner Victorian local, tastefully refurbished with a bar, smoke room, pool room, bowls pavilion and function room. Six real ales always available to complement quality home made food. Surprisingly large outdoor facilities include a bowling green and beer garden. Buses 504, 505, 506 & 507 stop in Newhampton Road West.

🏚️Q🌢🌓⊞♣🌑

Stile

3 Harrow Street, WV1 4PB

off Newhampton Road East (Fawdry Street jct)

🕐 12:00-23:00 Mon-Sat; 12:00-22:30 Sun

☎ (01902) 425336

Banks's Original, Bitter

Late Victorian pub which has been given local listed status. It has a small smoke room, club room and a public bar. The unusual L-shaped bowling green is overlooked by the old stable block dating back to the 1860's, the only reminder of a previous pub on this site. Can get very crowded on Wolves match days as Molineux is a short walk away. Buses 504, 505, 506, 507, 525 & 535A stop in Newhampton Road East.

🌢⊞

Summerhouse

283 Newhampton Road West, WV6 0RS

🕐 12:00-23:00 Mon-Sat; 12:00-22:30 Sun

☎ (01902) 658811

Banks's Original; Everards Tiger

The Summerhouse has quietly gone about serving its local community for the last 140 years, despite many changes that have happened around it. The secret of its survival is that it offers what its customers want and refuses to change to the latest fad. Long may it continue. Buses 504, 505, 506 & 507 stop nearby.

🏚️🌓🌢🌓⊞♣⊟

Wolverhampton: Wightwick

Fieldhouse

Perton Road, WV6 8DP

Near Wightwick Bank/Yew Tree Lane/ Mount Road jct.

🕐 16:00-23:00 Mon-Wed; 16:00-00:00 Thu-Fri; 16:00-00:00 Sat; 12:00-23:00 Sun

☎ (01902) 760011

Draught Bass; guest beer

Situated on the Staffordshire border, near to Wightwick Manor, the Fieldhouse was originally built as a beerhouse around 1780, serving the local farming community. It has two rooms, an L-shaped lounge and a tiny bar. The Wednesday curry night is the only time food is served. Ten minutes walk along Mount Road from 510 bus in Tettenhall Wood.

🏚️🌢⊞P

Woodsetton

Woodsetton has evolved from its rural origins into a suburban area. Up to the end of the 19th century Woodsetton remained a largely rural area between Dudley/Coseley, Sedgley/Tipton. The farmland has long since been swallowed up by suburbs.

Woodsetton (see Coseley map)

Park Inn

George Street, DY1 4LW
On A457, 200 yards from A4123

☼ 12:00-23:00 Mon-Sat; 12:00-22:30 Sun

☎ (01902) 661279

Holden's Mild, Bitter, Golden Glow, Special, seasonal beers

Home of Holden's brewery, bought by Edwin Alfred Holden in 1915. The main bar is light and airy with a raised dining area and large TV screen. From here there is access to a conservatory (available for functions) and a small games room. Competitively priced food is available daily. Buses from Dudley/Wolverhampton: 545 passes the pub; 125, 126 to Birmingham New Road then a 5 minute walk.

🌑◖♣P

Brewing in Wolverhampton

By the start of the twenty-first century, Wolverhampton had just one brewery left operating. The Wolverhampton & Dudley Brewery Chapel Ash is recognised and known as Banks's and is now a large regional brewery. With its recent expansions taking over Marstons, Camerons, Mansfield, Burntwood and Jennings and associated pubs, its coverage extends to a wide area. W&D was formed in 1890 to acquire the breweries of T Banks & Co of Meadow St Chapel Ash, C.C. Smith Fox Brewery of Wolverhampton, and George Thompson & Sons of Dudley. The Chapel Ash site was expanded and brewing is still carried on there today. In 1943 it took over Julia Hanson of Dudley where brewing continued until it was closed in 1991.

In the 1850's the town had many beer houses that brewed their own beer for sale, some supplying other outlets nearby. The demand was high as it was healthier to drink beer than the water that was available. Seeing an opportunity some malt houses began also to brew beer for the many pubs that did not brew their own. A few of those early breweries were Tettenhall Brewery 1841 to 1874, Wolverhampton Smithfield Brewery & South Staffordshire brewery both of Market Street who after several takeovers had both disappeared by 1920. Some others were Rogers & Calcutt, Thomas Russell, Frank Myatt and George Hill, all based in Wolverhampton. Outside Wolverhampton was Penn Brewery in Penn Common, the Wolverhampton District Brewery in Wesley Street Bradley, and James Cahill in Saint Matthews Street Heath Town.

Meanwhile in 1836 just over the town boundary in John Street Priestfield Ettingshall, the seeds of Wolverhampton's other major long lasting brewery were being planted. Born in 1816, William Butler at that time worked as a shingler in the nearby Thorneycroft Ironworks and also ran a grocers shop in John St. In 1840 he started brewing the beer he sold to his customers and his mates at the ironworks. By 1842 he had quit his job as a shingler to concentrate on his shop and small brewery at the rear.

Things clearly went well as by 1848 he had built a purpose built brewery in the yard at the rear using the local wells for his water. His beer was so much in demand that he employed a manager to run the grocers so that he could concentrate on brewing beer. At this time he also employed his first drayman to deliver beer by horse and cart to his expanding number of customers.

The business kept on expanding but by 1872 the wells had began to run dry and the need to relocate became urgent. His search was successful and he found a site in Wolverhampton at Springfields, which had a good water supply. It also had the advantage of being close to both the canal and both railway lines. The site was acquired and building commenced: by 1874 the brewery was in full production. During the 1880's he was joined by his sons William Junior and Edwin. He was hoping to retire but in 1886 son William died and he carried on working until he died in 1893. Edwin took over running the company but only 5 months later he died leaving the youngest son Samuel to carry on. Edwin remained on the board of directors until 1950.

Butlers Brewery continued to expand and thrive but in 1960 it was taken over by Mitchell's & Butlers of Cape Hill (a merger of Henry Mitchell and Butlers Crown Brewery in 1888). In 1961 they merged with Bass, Ratcliffe & Gretton to form Bass, Mitchell's & Butlers. Springfield brewery remained open and carried on brewing its beers including its wonderful Springfield bitter. The pubs still retained the Butlers signage until they either closed or underwent refurbishment, when they were signed as M & B outlets. By the late 1980s with a down turn of trade and rationalisation in the brewery industry, the future of brewing on the site was being discussed. After 115 years of brewing on the site it would continue to be used for distribution purposes only. The importance of the brewery and its buildings was recognised and part of the site, including the wonderful entrance gates, were given Statutory Listing. However due to poor maintenance and security the site became run down and in need of regeneration.

Springfield Brewery

Proposals were tabled in 1999 to encompass the listed parts of the site in to a proposed redevelopment scheme. After various schemes had been planned, abandoned or refused, in early 2004 it seemed that a plan incorporating the listed buildings was near to agreement. A Brewery Museum with its own Micro Brewery have been rumoured but the site was engulfed in a fire which it appeared had been started deliberately. It destroyed much of the old brewery buildings many of which were listed. It is hoped that restoration of some of the destroyed buildings may be possible when the site is redeveloped.

In more modern times Wolverhampton had two micro breweries. Holt Plant & Deakin brewed at the Ship & Rainbow (Brewery Tap) which for a short while became a Firkin Brewery. In 2001 the independent Goldthorn Brewery was opened by a local CAMRA member on the site in the former Sunbeam Car Factory. Despite brewing some excellent beer it suffered from lack of regular local outlets and closed in 2004.

Black Country Breweries

Banks's and Hanson's

Banks's Brewery, Park Brewery,
Wolverhampton, West Midlands, WV1 4NY
Tel (01902) 711811
Fax (01902) 429136
Website www.wdb.co.uk

Banks's was formed in 1890 by the amalgamation of three local companies. Hanson's was acquired in 1943 but its Dudley brewery was closed in 1991. Hanson's beers are now brewed in Wolverhampton, though its pubs retain the Hanson's livery. Banks's Original, the biggest-selling brand, is a fine example of West Midlands mild ale but the name was changed to give it a more 'modern' image. Beers from the closed Mansfield Brewery are now brewed at Wolverhampton.

Hanson's Mild Ale (OG 1035, ABV 3.3%)
A mid-to-dark brown mild with a malty roast flavour and aftertaste.

Mansfield Dark Mild (OG 1035, ABV 3.5%)

Riding Bitter (OG 1035, ABV 3.6%)

Banks's Original (OG 1036, ABV 3.5%)
An amber-coloured, well-balanced, refreshing session beer.

Banks's Bitter (OG 1038, ABV 3.8%)
A pale brown bitter with a pleasant balance of hops and malt. Hops continue from the taste through to a bitter-sweet aftertaste.

Mansfield Cask Ale (OG 1038, ABV 3.9%)

Batham's

Daniel Batham & Son Ltd, Delph Brewery, Delph Road, Brierley Hill,
West Midlands, DY5 2TN
Tel (01384) 77229
Fax (01384) 482292
Email info@bathams.com
Website www.bathams.com

A classic Black Country small brewery established in 1877. Tim and Matthew Batham represent the fifth generation to run the company. The Vine, one of the Black Country's most famous pubs, is also the site of the brewery. The company has 10 tied houses and supplies arond 25 other outlets. Such is the demand for Batham's Bitter that the beer is delivered in 54-gallon hogsheads. Seasonal beer: XXX (ABV 6.3%, December).

Mild Ale (OG 1036.5, ABV 3.5%)
A fruity, dark brown mild with a malty sweetness and a roast malt finish.

Best Bitter (OG 1043.5, ABV 4.3%)
A pale yellow, fruity, sweetish bitter, with a dry, hoppy finish. A good, light, refreshing beer.

Black Country

Black Country Ales, Old Bulls Head,
1 Redhall Road, Lower Gornal, Dudley,
West Midlands, DY3 2NU
Tel (01384) 231616
Fax (01384) 237513
Email info@blackcountryales.co.uk
Tours by arrangement except Sundays

The Brewery was set up in late 2004 by director Angus McMeeking and brewer Guy Perry. Guy was formally the brewer at nearby Sarah Hughes. The brewery is situated in part of the pub's original tower brewery, dating from 1834, which had produced its last brew in 1934. The plant is new. The already existing oak vessels that were installed in 1900 have been refurbished and brought into production. This gives a capacity of 50 barrels per week.

Bradley's Finest Golden (ABV 4.2%)
A straw-coloured beer, with a bold citrus hop aroma, balanced fruity sweetness and a refreshing hoppy aftertaste.

Pig on the Wall Mild (ABV 4.3%)
A chestnut brown beer in which a light fruity hops flavour moves to include roasted malt. Suggestions of chocolate and coffee undertones.

Fireside (ABV 5%)
A well-rounded premium amber bitter. Sweet and malty flavour leading to a good dry finish.

Highgate

Highgate Brewery Ltd, Sandymount Road, Walsall, West Midlands, WS1 3AP
Tel (01922) 644453
Fax (01922) 644471
Email info@highgatebrewery.com
Website www.highgatebrewery.com
Tours by arrangement

Built in 1898, Highgate was an independent brewery until 1938 when it was taken over by Mitchells & Butlers and subsequently became the smallest brewery in the Bass group. It was brought back into the independent sector in 1995 as the result of a management buy-out and was subsequently bought by Aston Manor in 2000. Some of the original equipment in the traditional Victorian brewery is still in use, but a new racking line and laboratory have been added along with a visitor facility. Highgate has now acquired 10 tied houses towards a target of 50, including the City Tavern, a restored Victorian ale house off Broad Street in Birmingham. Five of the tied houses serve cask-conditioned beer. Around 200 outlets are supplied. The company also has a major contract to supply Mitchells & Butlers pubs. Seasonal beer: Old Ale (ABV 5.3%, winter).

Dark Mild (OG 1036.8, ABV 3.6%)
A dark brown mild with a good balance of malt and hops, and traces of roast flavour following a malty aroma.

Special Bitter (OG 1037.8, ABV 3.8%)

Davenports Bitter (OG 1040.8, ABV 4%)
Based on the original Davenports recipe, this classic copper-coloured ale is full-bodied, with a palate rich in malt and fruit, balanced by a satisfying bitter finish.

Saddlers Best Bitter (OG 1043.8, ABV 4.3%)
A fruity, pale yellow bitter with a strong hop flavour and a light, refreshing bitter aftertaste.

Davenports Premium (OG 1046.8, ABV 4.6%)

For Coors:

M&B Mild (OG 1034.8, ABV 3.2%)

Holden's

Holden's Brewery Ltd, George Street, Woodsetton, Dudley, West Midlands, DY1 4LW
Tel (01902) 880051
Fax (01902) 665473
Email holdens.brewery@virgin.net
Website www.holdensbrewery.co.uk
Shop at Reception Mon-Fri 9-5 (beers & merchandise)
Tours by arrangement

A family brewery going back four generations, Holden's began life as a brew-pub when Edwin and Lucy took over the Park Inn (the brewery tap) in the 1920s; the inn has now been restored to its former Victorian heritage. Holden's also renovated a Grade II listed railway building in Codsall. The latest addition to the Holden's estate is the Waterfall in Blackheath. Holden's continues to grow with 21 tied pubs. It supplies some 60 other outlets.

Black Country Mild (OG 1037, ABV 3.7%)
A good, red/brown mild; a refreshing, light blend of roast malt, hops and fruit, dominated by malt throughout.

Black Country Bitter (OG 1039, ABV 3.9%)
A medium-bodied, golden ale; a light, well-balanced bitter with a subtle, dry, hoppy finish.

XB (OG 1042, ABV 4.1%)
A sweeter, slightly fuller version of the Bitter. Sold in a number of outlets under different names.

Golden Glow (OG 1045, ABV 4.4%)
A pale golden beer, with a subtle hop aroma plus gentle sweetness and a light hoppiness.

Special (OG 1052, ABV 5.1%)
A sweet, malty, full-bodied amber ale with hops to balance in the taste and in the good, bitter-sweet finish.

Sarah Hughes

Sarah Hughes Brewery, 129 Bilston Street, Sedgley, West Midlands, DY3 1JE
Tel (01902) 883381
Fax (01902) 884020
Tours by prior arrangement

A traditional Black Country tower brewery, established in 1921. The original grist case and rare open-topped copper add to the ambience of the Victorian brewhouse and give a unique character to the brews. Future plans involve additional seasonal beers, expanding fermenting space to cope with demand and adding a full range of bottle-conditioned beers. One pub, the Beacon Hotel, is owned. Seasonal beer: Snow Flake (ABV 8%). Bottle-conditioned beer: Dark Ruby.

Pale Amber (OG 1038, ABV 4%)
A well-balanced beer, initially slightly sweet but with hops close behind.

Surprise Bitter (OG 1048, ABV 5%)
A bitter-sweet, medium-bodied, hoppy ale with some malt.

Dark Ruby (OG 1058, ABV 6%)
A dark ruby strong ale with a good balance of fruit and hops, leading to a pleasant, lingering hops and malt finish.

Olde Swan

Olde Swan Brewery, 87-89 Halesowen Road, Netherton, Dudley, West Midlands, DY2 9PY
Tel (01384) 253075
Tours by arrangement

A famous and much-loved brew-pub, best known in the old days as 'Ma Pardoe's', after the matriarch who ruled it for years. The pub has been licensed since 1835 and the present brewery and pub were built in 1863. Brewing continued until 1988 and restarted in 2001. The plant brews primarily for the on-site pub with some beer available to the trade. Some 20 outlets are supplied. Seasonal beer: Black Widow (ABV 6.7%, winter).

Original (OG 1034, ABV 3.5%)
Straw-coloured light mild, smooth but tangy, and sweetly refreshing with a faint hoppiness.

Dark Swan (OG 1041, ABV 4.2%)
Smooth, sweet dark mild with very late roast malt in the finish.

Entire (OG 1043, ABV 4.4%)
Faintly hoppy, amber premium bitter with sweetness persistent throughout.

Bumble Hole Bitter
(OG 1052, ABV 5.2%)
Sweet, smooth amber ale with hints of astringency in the finish.

Toll End

Toll End Brewery, Waggon & Horses,
131 Toll End Road, Tipton, West Midlands, DY4 0ET
Tel (0121) 502 6453

A two-barrel brewery was installed at the pub in November 2004. Various seasonal and occasional beers are also brewed.

Black Bridge (ABV 4.6%)
A chestnut-coloured ale flavoured with Cascade hops.

PA/Phoebe's Ale (ABV 4.7%)
Very light hoppy beer.

Windsor Castle

Windsor Castle Brewery Ltd, t/a Sadler's Ales,
7 Stourbridge Road, Lye, Stourbridge,
West Midlands, DY9 7DG
Tel (01384) 897809
Fax (01384) 893666
Email johnsadler@windsorcastlebrewery.com
Website www.windsorcastlebrewery.com
Shop 5-10pm daily (not Sun or Mon)
Tours by arrangement

Nathaniel Sadler opened the original brewery in 1900 adjacent to the Windsor Castle Inn, Oldbury. Although brewing ceased in 1927, his son John Caleb Nathaniel Sadler, who was brought up in the brewery, passed on all he knew to the current John Sadler. John and his son Chris have reopened the brewery in its new location, continuing the brewing tradition of the Sadler family. There is an off-licence on site.

Jack's Ale (ABV 3.8%)
Light, hoppy beer with a crisp and zesty lemon undertone.

Bitter Ale (ABV 4.3%)
Smooth, refreshing session bitter with underlying flavours of honey and caramel, with a complex hop character.

Worcester Sorcerer (ABV 4.3%)
Pale beer, light and refreshing yet smooth and fruity with hints of mint and lemon. Floral aroma and crisp bitterness combine to make a balanced and clean-tasting beer.

1900 Original (ABV 4.5%)
Dark malty bitter with a light hoppy aroma and a dry, lingering finish.

IPA (ABV 4.8%)
Classic India Pale Ale, light, tangy and bitter with a distinctive refreshing aftertaste.

Staffordshire Breweries

The following breweries fall within the area covered by the Black Country branches, but are located just over the county boundary in Staffordshire.

Beowulf

Beowulf Brewing Co,
Chasewater Country Park, Pool Road, Brownhills, Staffordshire, WS8 7NL
Tel/Fax (01543) 454067
Email beowulfbrewing@yahoo.co.uk
Tours Small tours by arrangement

After six successful years producing Birmingham's only cask beer in a converted shop, Beowulf moved to new premises in 2003. The beers appear as guest ales in the central region and across the country. Seasonal beers: autumn and winter – Hurricane (ABV 4%), Glutlusty (ABV 4.5%), Finn's Hall Porter (ABV 4.7%), Blizzard (ABV 5%), Grendal's Winter Ale (ABV 5.8%); spring and summer – Wergild (ABV 4.3%), Fifty Winters (ABV 4.4%), Wuffa (ABV 4.5%), Gold Work (ABV 5.1%). Bottling is imminent.

Beorma (OG 1038, ABV 3.9%)
A pale session ale with a malty hint of fruit giving way to a lingering bitterness.

Noble Bitter (OG 1039, ABV 4%)
Gold colour, fruity aroma, hoppy taste with a dry finish.

Wiglaf (OG 1043, ABV 4.3%)
A golden bitter, with a malty flavour married to a pleasing bitterness, with three hop varieties used.

Chasewater Bitter (OG 1043, ABV 4.4%)

Swordsman (OG 1045, ABV 4.5%)
Pale gold, light fruity aroma, tangy hoppy flavour. Faintly hoppy finish.
Dragon Smoke Stout (OG 1048, ABV 4.7%)

Heroes Bitter (OG 1046, ABV 4.7%)
Gold colour, malt aroma, hoppy taste but sweetish finish.

Mercian Shine (OG 1048, ABV 5%)
Pale gold colour, citrus flavour with a full body and hoppy, dry finish

Enville

Enville Ales Ltd, Enville Brewery, Cox Green, Enville, Stourbridge, West Midlands, DY7 5LG
Tel (01384) 873728
Fax (01384) 873770
Email info@envilleales.com
Website www.envilleales.com
Tours by arrangement for small groups only

Enville is based on a picturesque Victorian farm complex. Using the same water source as the original Village Brewery (closed in 1919), the beers also incorporate more than three tons of honey annually, and originally used recipes passed down from the proprietor's great-great aunt. Six outlets are supplied. Seasonal beer: Gothic (ABV 5.2%, Oct-March).

Chainmaker Mild (OG 1037, ABV 3.6%)
A classic style mild, dark and well balanced with a hop aroma and underlying sweetness which, combined with the smooth malty finish, makes it an excellent example of a traditional Black Country mild.

Nailmaker Mild (OG 1041, ABV 4%)
With a more defined hop aroma and higher gravity than its counterpart this mild enjoys a certain degree of sweetness associated with traditional mild yet gives a drier finish.

White (OG 1041, ABV 4.2%)
A clean, well balanced, golden, sweet bitter, light in flavour.

Saaz (OG 1042, ABV 4.2%)
Golden lager-style beer. Lager bite but with more taste and lasting bitterness. The malty aroma is late arriving but the bitter finish, balanced by fruit and hops, compensates.

Ale (OG 1044, ABV 4.5%)
Pale gold to yellow. Very sweet start but with a bite. Heathery almost whisky hints give way to a thirst-quenching hoppiness and pleasing end.

Old Porter (OG 1044, ABV 4.5%)
A traditional style Porter, dark in appearance and offering a complex mix of roast malt and fruit flavours with a degree of sweetness giving way to a dry finish.

Ginger (OG 1045, ABV 4.6%)
A refreshing beer made with root ginger extract.

Kinver

Kinver Brewery, 2 Fairfield Drive, Kinver, Staffordshire, DY7 6EW
Tel 07715 842679
Email kinvercave@aol.com
Website www.kinverbrewery.co.uk
Tours by arrangement

The brewery was founded in 2004 by two CAMRA members. The five-barrel plant produces three regular beers in a unit on a small industrial estate off the High Street. Seasonal ales, including a Maibock, a Mild and a summer ale are produced. Seasonal beer: Over the Sledge (ABV 7.5%) Pale strong Christmas beer.

Edge Best Bitter (ABV 4.2%)
Pale and hoppy.

Pail Ale (ABV 4.4%)

Caveman Strong Bitter (ABV 5.2%)
Brewed with Crystal malt and Goldings hops. Smooth, rounded and easily drinkable, keeping its strength well hidden. The beer to drink before clubbing.

Over the Edge (ABV 7.6%)
A strong pale golden ale, with a powerful taste and hop flavour. Brewed with all pale Maris Otter with a proportion of wheat, and a single hop variety.

Do you feel passionately about your pint?
Then why not join CAMRA

Just fill in the application form (or a photocopy of it) and the Direct Debit form on the next page to receive three months' membership FREE!

If you wish to join but do not want to pay by Direct Debit, please fill in the application form below and send a cheque, payable to CAMRA to: CAMRA, 230 Hatfield Road, St Albans, Hertfordshire, AL1 4LW.

Please check www.camra.org.uk or phone 01727 867201 for current membership prices

☐ Single Membership (UK & EU) £____
☐ For under-26 Membership £____
☐ For 60 and over Membership £____

For partners' joint membership add £____ (for concessionary rates both members must be eligible for the membership rate).
Life membership information is available on request.

If you join by Direct Debit you will receive three months' membership extra, free!

Title_____ Surname_____

Forename(s)_____

Address_____

_____

Postcode_____ Date of Birth_____

Email address_____

Signature_____

Partner's details if required

Title_____ Surname_____

Forename(s)_____

Date of Birth_____

Email address_____

Please tick here ☐ if you would like to receive occasional emails from CAMRA (at no point will your details be released to a third party).

Instruction to your Bank or Building Society to pay by Direct Debit

Please fill in the form and send to: Campaign for Real Ale Ltd. 230 Hatfield Road, St. Albans, Herts. AL1 4LW

Name and full postal address of your Bank or Building Society

Originator's Identification Number

| 9 | 2 | 6 | 1 | 2 | 9 |

To The Manager   Bank or Building Society

Address

Postcode

Name (s) of Account Holder (s)

Bank or Building Society account number

Branch Sort Code

Reference Number

FOR CAMRA OFFICIAL USE ONLY
This is not part of the instruction to your Bank or Building Society

Membership Number

Name

Postcode

Instruction to your Bank or Building Society
Please pay CAMRA Direct Debits from the account detailed on this Instruction subject to the safeguards assured by the Direct Debit Guarantee. I understand that this instruction may remain with CAMRA and, if so, will be passed electronically to my Bank/Building Society

Signature(s)

Date

Banks and Building Societies may not accept Direct Debit Instructions for some types of account

- - - - - - - - - - ✂ - - - - - - - - - - - - - - detached and retained this section

This Guarantee should be detached and retained by the payer.

The Direct Debit Guarantee

- This Guarantee is offered by all Banks and Building Societies that take part in the Direct Debit Scheme. The efficiency and security of the Scheme is monitored and protected by your own Bank or Building Society.

- If the amounts to be paid or the payment dates change CAMRA will notify you 7 working days in advance of your account being debited or as otherwise agreed.

- If an error is made by CAMRA or your Bank or Building Society, you are guaranteed a full and immediate refund from your branch of the amount paid.

- You can cancel a Direct Debit at any time by writing to your Bank or Building Society. Please also send a copy of your letter to us.